The Most Gracious Gazillionaire

Volume One
Be Yourself and Walk in Purpose

A True Poetic Journey on Launching into "... the Deep" and Finding Purpose

SIMONE A. CLARKE

Copyright © 2019 by Simone A. Clarke

All rights reserved. This book or any portion thereof may not be reproduced or used in any manner whatsoever without the express written permission of the publisher except for the use of brief quotations in a book review.

Printed in the United States of America
First edition January 28, 2019
Revised edition October 25, 2020
ISBN-13: 978-976-96261-7-1

Simone A. Clarke
Jamaica
simoneaclarkethepoet@gmail.com

This book is a memoir. It reflects the author's present recollection of experiences overtime. Some names and characteristics have been changed, some events have been compressed, and some dialogue has been recreated.

Cover by Mrs. Jae – Anne Bell

Scriptures marked KJV are taken from the KING JAMES VERSION (KJV): KING JAMES VERSION; public domain.

Scriptures marked (AMP) are taken from the AMPLIFIED BIBLE (AMP): Scripture taken from the AMPLIFIED® BIBLE, Copyright © 1954, 1958, 1962, 1964, 1965, 1987 by the Lockman Foundation Used by Permission. (www.Lockman.org)

Scriptures marked (ESV) are taken from the THE HOLY BIBLE, ENGLISH STANDARD VERSION (ESV): Scriptures taken from THE HOLY BIBLE, ENGLISH STANDARD VERSION ® Copyright© 2001 by Crossway, a publishing ministry of Good News Publishers. Used by permission.

Scriptures marked (ISV) are taken from the INTERNATIONAL STANDARD VERSION (ISV): Scripture taken from INTERNATIONAL STANDARD VERSION, copyright© 1996-2008 by the ISV Foundation. All rights reserved internationally.

Scripture quotation marked (KJ 2000) are taken from the KING JAMES 2000 BIBLE, copyright © 2001 by Robert A. Couric, Editor. Used by permission.

Scriptures marked (NIV) are taken from the NEW INTERNATIONAL VERSION (NIV): Scripture taken from THE HOLY BIBLE, NEW INTERNATIONAL VERSION ®. Copyright© 1973, 1978, 1984, 2011 by Biblica, Inc.™. Used by permission of Zondervan

Scripture quotations marked (NKJV) are taken from The New King James Version. Copyright © 1982 by Thomas Nelson, Inc. Used by permission. All rights reserved.

Scriptures marked (NLT) are taken from the HOLY BIBLE, NEW LIVING TRANSLATION (NLT): Scriptures taken from the HOLY BIBLE, NEW LIVING TRANSLATION, Copyright© 1996, 2004, 2007 by Tyndale House Foundation. Used by permission of Tyndale House Publishers, Inc., Carol Stream, Illinois 60188. All rights reserved. Used by permission.

DEDICATION

This volume is dedicated to my mother

Ivy Elizabeth Lynch-Clarke

Who lived a life of purpose

May 20, 1954 – January 31, 2018.

To my beloved daughter Gianna and all the children who call me "Aunty",
enjoy the gift of God's grace and walk in His purpose.

I make known the end from the beginning, from ancient times, what is still to come. I say, 'My purpose will stand, and I will do all that I please.'

Isaiah 46:10 (NIV)

CONTENTS

Dedication iii
Contents v
Acknowledgments ix
Foreword xi
Introduction 1
To Walk in Your Purpose, "Launch Out into the Deep!" 7
   "Submit the Letter…" 9
   "Launch out into the Deep!" 13
   Train Ride with the S.T.A.R.R.S – 15
   Wall Street 15
   Train Ride with the S.T.A.R.R.S – 17
   It's Showtime! 17
   Train Ride with the S.T.A.R.R.S – 20
   Shock Level Elevated to Eight 20
Your Calling and Purpose 23
   Your Purpose 25
   Your Calling 27
   Appreciate Your Calling 29
   Appreciate Your Gift 31
   Humility – Essential to Walking in Purpose 32
   "Ask and It Shall Be Given" 33
   Exercise Your Faith 34

Trust His Strategy 35

Trusting in "…..the Deep"……………………………….. 37

"In God Put Your Trust"..39

Trusting in "…the Deep" – Part One 43

Trusting in "…the Deep" – Part Two 45

Watch Me Work..48

Fear or Faith 50

Seasons 52

The Cup on the Window Sill 53

This is Only Temporary...54

Pruning...56

Refining..57

Be Faithful 58

Finish Strong! 59

Trusting in "the Deep" – Finale 60

Trust = Faith + Action...61

The Girl Who Lived Between the Hills and the Town is Thankful.. 65

Weathering "…the Deep" – Coat Weight 67

Weathering "…the Deep" – Butt of a Joke.......................68

Thanksgiving Day 70

Thanksgiving Dinner...71

Thank You 72

Lord, We Give You Thanks...73

Christmas is Here! 74
Happy New Year – Write the Vision 78
Happy Birthday – Smile! 79
Friends 80
Grateful to the Men 82
Grateful to the Ladies 85
Grateful to All 86
Be Yourself and Walk in Purpose 87
Your Name and Purpose 89
Rare Diamond 90
We Are SPECIAL 91
I Am Loved 93
Jesus a Mi Friend*   Jesus is My Friend   (Dub poem)
.... 96
Be Yourself and Walk in Purpose 97
Be Tankful for Woo Yu Bi (Jamaican Patois) Be Thankful for Who You Are 98
Take Me Out of Your Box 102
Diving Deeper in "...the Deep" – Part One 105
Diving Deeper in "...the Deep" – Part Two 107
Diving Deeper in "...the Deep" – Part Three 109
Diving Deeper in "...the Deep" – Finale 111
A Pleasant Administrator and Team Leader 113
It Is Well With Mother 115
Glossary **119**

Notes 123

The Most Gracious Gazillionaire Series 141

About the Author 142

ACKNOWLEDGMENTS

This book would not have been possible without my Heavenly Father who demonstrated the "limitless riches of his grace" to me while I was studying in New York City, and as I wrote this volume of poetry. Lord, I thank You for all the people You had in place to help me.

I am forever grateful that after returning from the United States, I got two years to spend with my mother, Mrs. Ivy Clarke, before she died. She was very supportive of my studies and got the opportunity to read my manuscripts and the first published volume. I also owe a huge debt of gratitude to my daughter Gianna, my father Mr. Alfred Clarke, my sisters, Lyssa-Ann and Lauri-Ann, and Dr. Dacia Dixon. I thank you all for your patience and generosity. A special thank you to Miss Annmarie Reid, Ms. Myrna Currie, Ms. Jennifer McDonald and family who responded to God's prompting and made it possible for me to have accommodation for my final year of study. To my other relatives and friends in Jamaica, Pennsylvania, Florida, Georgia, Wisconsin, New Jersey and New York, I appreciate your prayers and support.

My sincere gratitude to the following departments of Brooklyn College of The City University of New York: The Office of International Student and Scholar Services; The Enrollment Services Center; The Financial Aid Department; The Brooklyn College Foundation and The Scholarship Office; The Department of Public Safety; The Information Technology Service; The Childhood, Bilingual and Special Education Departments and The Residence Hall. Thank you all for the assistance given throughout my studies.

I am also extremely grateful to the following people who assisted me with this book: Mrs. M. Nelson for a quiet and cozy place to rest and give birth to my poems. Mr. and Mrs. Bell of Brooklyn and Lauri-Ann Clarke, who ensured I was properly equipped to write after graduation; Miss Myrna Currie, who made recommendations about the first draft of my poems; Dr. Marlegrecy N'Ovec, an editor whose wisdom and critique became encouragement for me to strive for excellence and Rev. Lennox Scarlett, for writing the foreword of this volume. To my reviewers: Mrs. Lyssa-Ann Clarke-Nelson, Mrs. Michelle Blake and Ms. Gloria Evadney Ellis; my Illustrator, Mrs. Jae-Anne Bell; Marketing Consultant, Mrs. Carol Wray and Self-Publishing Consultant, Mrs. Marsha Malcolm, thanks a million!

Finally, my sincere gratitude to the following churches for demonstrating God's grace through their kindness: World Changers Church, Brooklyn and The Brooklyn Tabernacle Church. A special thank you to the leaders and members of Family Church on the Rock, Kingston, Jamaica, for praying and encouraging me throughout my studies.

FOREWORD

The desire to tell a story of coming to absolute dependence on God in spite of clear and present uncertainties speaks to a faith that is grounded and certain. That's how I've known Simone Clarke, a resolute and determined young woman. I shared only a small part of this early journey; as while her pastor for eight years at the Salisbury Plain United Church, she showed signs of a Christian maturity well beyond her teenage years, and was usually called upon to lead in worship and youth work; share a faith story of God's hand in her life, or in some other way. While her usual willingness to challenge her peers and others on matters of faith and belief were not always met with immediate and obvious evidence of God's providence in areas of her life, Simone's constant quest at self-determination bolstered by God's leading was clear. The chronicling of her journey has therefore not come as a surprise.

This book, *The Most Gracious Gazillionaire ...Be Yourself and Walk in Purpose*, provides a valuable window on information assurance and covers the necessary components of a journey that is built on real-life experience of questions, fear, frustrations, disappointments, and hope transformed into belief, trust and confidence in the Most Gracious Gazillionaire.

Because of its uniqueness, this autobiographical journey told through anthological lenses, provides readers with a glimpse of a relationship shared between Simone and her God. Clearly, Christians have their own stories and will tell them differently. But the truth of the matter is — and this is in spite of those fine religious people who attempt to placate God by means of laws and rules and traditions and customs — that Simone's story is where she stood and that is what we celebrate.

The Most Gracious Gazillionaire comes against the background of trying times in Simone's life: doubt, divorce, and death of a loved one. As Christians, we are drawn into the story, because it becomes our story too. Because whether it's physical pain or mental or emotional anguish, material loss or excruciating sorrow, this does not separate us from God, nor alter our relationship with God. However, as Simone points out, it is when we accept and cling to what God has done for us through Christ, irrespective of our own human feelings and frailties, that the very conflicts that beset us and may even threaten to destroy us, become God's tools to grind and polish and temper our spirits and prepare us for deeper wisdom and service, as we come into our purpose.

Rev. Lennox Scarlett
Former Minister of Salisbury Plain United Church
Minister of Oakland - Scotland Community Church
Ontario, Canada

Many are the plans in the mind of a man,
But it is the purpose of the Lord that will stand.

Proverbs 19:21
English Standard Version (ESV)

The purpose in a man's heart is like deep water, but a man of understanding will draw it out.

Proverbs 20:5 (ESV)

INTRODUCTION

New York City, November 2014:
Approximately six months after graduating from Brooklyn College of The City University of New York I cried, "Somebody! Please! Help me! Help me now!" It was the anniversary month of my one -year divorce, a climax to a seven-year separation, and I was about to give birth to "Peace". About an hour before "Peace", I had pushed out "Schemes" in anger. "Schemes" underwent intense surgeries over the following months and had its name changed to "Shot Gun Words" as I learned to "Be Like Joseph". Within a year, more than 150 poems and dialogues incorporating biblical verses were born.

The Island of Jamaica, January 2016 – August 2018:
On January 27, 2016, I returned to my country and within twelve days was employed in a temporary position as a teacher. I added and edited poems on weekends and, anxious to see my first book on Amazon, I published volume two as volume one in August. I had forgotten the instruction written in my journal, having been given by my Heavenly Father eight months earlier, to introduce the poems "slowly as feeding a babe." On the morning of August 26, 2016, while at a training seminar for a new job offer, I was in high spirits seeing my book on Amazon; however, a few hours later, I received news that the start date of the job would be rescheduled. The date was confirmed for most of the other trainees a few weeks later, but unfortunately, I was not offered the job.

That loss, however, gave me the opportunity to be with my mother, Mrs. Ivy Clarke, who had just retired from the teaching profession as a high school principal. She was honoured at a retirement function at the school on January 26, 2017, three months before being diagnosed with colon cancer. I believed the cancer would have miraculously disappeared as the cysts in my breasts did in 2015; however, after two surgeries in May and June 2017, her condition worsened. On January 25, 2018, one year after my mom's retirement function, I left work earlier than usual and headed home, not knowing it would be my mom's last day there. My dad and I took her to the hospital, where she died on January 31, 2018 of Pulmonary Embolism and Metastatic Colon Cancer. She was a beautiful wife and mother, and an extraordinary educator for 42 years.

By March 2018, I was wrestling with anger because my life seemed to be going in a direction I had not planned. I then began questioning whether the title of my book was appropriate. How can I call the Heavenly Father "The Most Gracious Gazillionaire"? Though my relationship with Him had deepened and I had experienced his abundant mercy and grace, I began doubting whether "All things work together for good to them that love God, to them who are called according to his purpose." (Romans 8:28 KJV). The anger intensified to bitterness by June as I had been waiting nearly two and a half years to receive my correct salary. I was being paid approximately 40% of what I should have been earning. Despite my trials, my Heavenly Father ensured my needs were met, demonstrating that He was my source and not a salary.

One Saturday evening as I sat near the stream at my parents' home, I became very conscious that I was surrounded by lush fruit trees and green grass, which were not angry or complaining, but resting. Some of those trees had gone through hurricanes and storms and were still standing. I had to "Be Like Joseph" as my Heavenly Father reassured me of His love, mercy and tender care. I made my mind up to continue referring to Him in my poems as "The Most Gracious Gazillionaire."

According to the complete and unabridged 2012 digital edition of the *Collins English Dictionary*, "A gazillionaire is a person who is enormously rich." In the commentary of *The Everyday Life Bible, Amplified Version* (2006), grace, as appeared in John 1:17 and Titus 2:11, is defined as "Unearned, undeserved, unmerited favor and spiritual blessings." I refer to our Heavenly Father as "The Most Gracious Gazillionaire" because His loving-kindness and tender mercies cannot be measured, and His grace, which came by Jesus Christ, is the greatest expression of unearned, undeserved, unmerited favor and blessings given to all people.

The *Most Gracious Gazillionaire Series* covers three volumes:

Volume One – *Be Yourself and Walk in Purpose*
Volume Two – *"My Grace is Sufficient for You…"*

Volume Three – *Experience the "Limitless Riches of His Grace"*
In this volume, *Be Yourself and Walk in Purpose*, the author, "The Girl Who Lived Between the Hills and the Town" hears from "The Most Gracious Gazillionaire" and decides to follow His instructions to "Submit the Letter…" and "Launch out into the Deep" to study in New York City. After a ballad entitled "Train Ride with the S.T.A.R.RS", she begins to ask about her true calling and purpose and soon realizes that the journey to purpose is one of trusting, pruning and refining.

"The Girl Who Lived Between the Hills and the Town" then uses the poem "Weathering the Deep – Coat Weight" and "Weathering the Deep – Butt of a Joke" to share her experience about the winter seasons of New York City and that in the midst of difficulties, you can find humor in your situation. In the poems "Grateful to the Men" and "Grateful to the Women" she expresses thanks to the people who assisted her throughout her studies. Coincidentally, those people had names or personalities that were synonymous with major characters of stories in the Bible. Their help, she believed, was a true expression of God's grace and a way of telling her that she was in His purpose. In the final section of this volume, "The Most Gracious Gazillionaire" encourages the Girl and others to "Be Yourself and Walk in Purpose" and then uses the Jamaican dialect to encourage us to be thankful. The author then describes how she was guided into her Heavenly Father's purpose and ends the book with two poems dedicated to her mother.

I strongly recommend that the poems be read in the sequence given. They are based on the real-life journey of the author, who hopes that the poems will inspire others to "Launch out into the Deep", be themselves and walk in purpose.

SIMONE A. CLARKE

To Walk in Your Purpose, "Launch Out into the Deep!"

Gazillionaire - A person who is enormously rich. In my poems, The Heavenly Father is called **The Most Gracious Gazillionaire** because His loving kindness and tender mercies are immeasurable, and His grace, which came by Jesus Christ is the greatest expression of unearned, undeserved, unmerited favour and blessings given to all people.

"Submit the Letter..."

2002 – 2003
A great year for
The Girl Who Lived Between the Hills and the Town.
She walked down the aisle on cloud nine
To marry her beau of five years;
Received her undergraduate degree;
She graduated!
Had a nine-and-a-half-pound baby girl
She was elated!

About three and a half years later
The Girl Who Lived Between the Hills and the Town
Awoke in panic;
What had she seen in her dream?
Her wedding photo
Torn down the middle?
She softly prayed
Though she wanted to scream.

As she got dressed for work February 2006
She felt a change brewing;
A still, small voice said,
'"Beauty for Ashes"
I love you.'
Unaware those words were spoken in preparation
For a marriage which in three months
Would be ablaze with a separation
And would leave grey ashes
Too weighty to mention.

Though the burn
Caused much pain
She trusted her Lord

To give her "Beauty for Ashes"
For in His will she would remain.

As the Girl slept in the dark
December 2006,
The words "Feed My Sheep"
Rang in her ears;
The echo it left
Made her remember
The meaning of her name,
Which in Hebrew means "Loud"
And "One who hears."

"Feed My Sheep."
A command given three times
By Jesus to Simon Peter in the Bible;
A command now given to
The Girl Who Lived Between the Hills and the Town;
A command she pondered for months to comprehend;
Was she to preach like Peter?
How?
Where?
When?

The Girl read her Bible every day before
Heading to work;
And in January 2008 she heard,
"I AM sending you to New York..."

Though what she heard
Did not make much sense,
As she read the Bible,
Her desire to study in that city
Became more intense.

Three years passed,

And on January 24, 2011 she clearly heard,
"New York is about to come to pass…"
She reasoned in her mind
About how things would work
And in May 2011,
The still, small voice said,
"Submit the letter and watch me work."

Would the Girl obey what she heard
And trust the Lord to lead her?
Or ignore the voice
And allow fear to control her?

She allowed fear to control her
And postponed the submission of her resignation letter.
The passion she had for her work faded,
Unaware, the grace to do that job had ended.

The Girl continued reading her Bible
Listened to messages on "Faith"
Believed it was her Heavenly Father's voice she heard
And whatever He impressed on her heart or spoke,
She opened her journal and wrote:

"Be not wise in your own eyes…"
Stop reasoning about how things will work to the end.
Turn away from wanting to do your thing;
Allow Me to direct you
I AM your King.

I placed the idea of going back to school in your heart
For it best suits you and your purpose.
I love you;
I will lead you;
Don't be stressed
Or become anxious.

I will direct you to the school which suits you.
I Am more accurate
Than your GPS systems.
Trust Me!
Follow My directions!
For, "Many are the plans in the mind of a man
But it is only the purpose of the Lord that will stand."

Forget about what was said
Is said
And will be said about you.
Just do what I tell you to do;
This stage is a process of training and discipline
For the purpose I have for you.

Yes!
All your props will be removed
And it may seem frightening at the start,
Just lean and rely on Me,
From you I will never depart.
"Be not wise in your own eyes…"
Go where I send you;
Get ready, start packing!
Go ahead!
Just trust Me
I "…will not leave or forsake you."

The Girl Who Lived Between the Hills and the Town
Submitted the resignation letter for August of that year;
Began a journey of purpose with The One,
Unconditional with his love and care,
Her Most Gracious Heavenly Father,
"The Most Gracious Gazillionaire."

"Launch out into the Deep!"

Do you want to catch fish?
Move the boat from the seashore and
"Launch out into the Deep!"

But the tides are too high!
I don't want to die!
Many sharks and whales out there!

"Launch out into the Deep!"

How will I go to school?
No tuition in sight
Will need lunch money to catch a bite.

"Launch out into the Deep!"

I have a business plan
All I need is for someone to give me a hand.

"Launch out into the Deep!"

Loneliness has consumed me,
No friend
To sit with and have tea.

"Launch out into the Deep!"

Launching "Out into the Deep"
Will require steadfast trust in The Lord;
The waves may seem rough;
Swim!
Relax and float…
You will not drown!

Exercise your faith and believe!
Go!
Walk in your purpose!

"Launch out into the Deep!"

Train Ride with the S.T.A.R.R.S – Wall Street[1]

The Girl Who Lived Between the Hills and the Town
Began seeking sponsorship for her studies
October 2011.
She stopped in Pennsylvania first,
Visited relatives there,
Then rode on a bus for two hours, "...into the Deep,"
New York City,
"The city that never sleeps."

She walked quickly to the subways;
A steel drum musician filled the air
With a tune by the mighty calypso bird;
People of every nationality
Waited for their trains
And only the pulsating beats could be heard.

"There is a train approaching the station,
Please move away from the platform."
The Girl pulled the suitcase quickly unto the train;
The bell rang
The door closed;
The announcer said,
"The next stop is Wall Street."

The Girl went into shock;
"Wall Street!
Like the one on TV!

---

[1] All the activities in the series "Train Ride with the S.T.A.R.R.S took place during the time the author lived in New York City.

Kiss mi neck!"[2]
Her patois language quickly
Revealing her native country.

"This is Wall Street," said the announcer.
Men and women in well-pressed suits
Exited the train quickly and with confidence.
She suppressed her excitement
And hummed this song
As the train
Approached the next station:

"I am riding with Jesus on the New York Subway[3]
I am singing and shouting on the New York Subway
I stopped at the Wall Street station
But college is my destination
I am riding with Jesus
On the New York Subway...."

---

[22]"Kiss mi neck" (Kiss my neck) – A Jamaican Creole (patois) expression of surprise.

[33]Sung to the tune of "I am riding with Jesus on the Alleluia train"

Train Ride with the S.T.A.R.R.S – It's Showtime!

"Ladies and gentlemen,
Will you help me, please?
God bless you."
Coins and dollar notes
Were dropped in the beggar's hat
As he walked through the car.
His only response was,
"Thank you very much.
Thank you very much."

He got off at the next stop
And walked to the next car;
That was the Girl's next shock!
She realised that was the man's reality,
It was not an act.

If that man was conscious
That he was created
To be one of God's Gracious S.T.A.R.R.S,
His accepted friend "Shame"
Would have had to admire him from afar.
If he knew he was created to be
A Gracious, Smart, Talented, Advisable, Respectful and Righteous Steward,
He would have exited the train
With his face showing Hope,
Hope of a reward.

"Excuse me, ladies and gentlemen,
I am selling snacks."
The Girl Who Lived Between the Hill and the Town
Watched as a little boy exchanged

Each of his snacks for a dollar.
The Girl was happy for him;
Learning to hustle at such a young age;
He was in training for a larger business
And would soon fly from his cage.

"Ladies and gentlemen,
It's Showtime!"
"I am Peter!" and "I am Paul!"[4]
There were oohs! aahs! and claps
As the two showed off their skills and break danced.
In her mind the Girl exclaimed,
"Head top and pole dance![5]
Pon di train!
Big up yourself, mi yutes![6]
How entertaining for $2.50.
I love this route!"

---

[44]Names changed to protect their identities.
[55]"Head top" – A Jamaican Creole expression referring to dancing on one's head. "Pole dance" – Dancing on a pole, as a stripper.
[66]"Big up yourself, mi yutes!" – A Jamaican Creole extending kudos to the young men. Literally, "Give yourselves praise, my youths!"

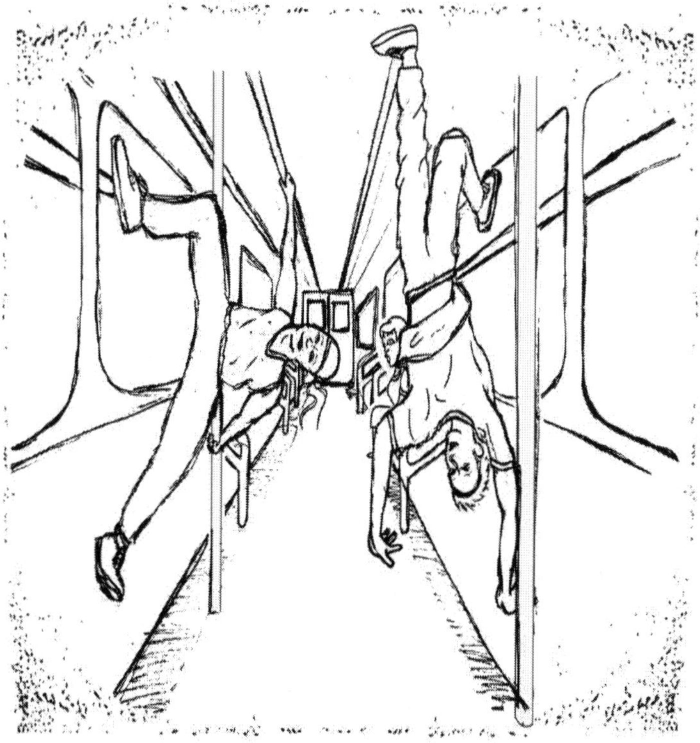

Train Ride with the S.T.A.R.R.S – Shock Level Elevated to Eight

"Your mama!"
"Don't you say anything about my mama!"
"Look at your phone!
That is out of style!"
"Get with the program, girrrrrl!
Go get a wig!
Your hair is dry and needs oil!"

The man and woman were about to fight;
The Girl Who Lived Between the Hills and the Town
Looked on in fright!
Her shock level had now elevated to eight!
She was desperate to reach her gate.
The announcer said, "The next stop is Franklin Avenue."
The woman needing the hairdo exited;
The Girl was thankful a fight was averted.

"Ladies and gentlemen, Jesus loves you!
He is the God of our Salvation!
Believe in Him!
He is coming soon!"
This lady was ignored;
She did not get the same attention
As the beggar, businessman, dancers
Nor the two throwing words;
She was brave and stood alone
As she warned about the Lord's coming
 Knowing it was soon time to go home.

The Girl Who Lived Between the Hills and the Town
Was getting weary;
Her car was almost empty

And then she heard it,
"The next and last stop is Brooklyn College."
Her heart raced...
"This is the last stop.
Please leave the train.
Thank you for riding...."

"I know that You can do all things, and that no thought or purpose of Yours can be restrained or thwarted."

Job 42:2 (AMP)

Your Calling and Purpose

"Look carefully then how you walk!
Live purposefully and worthily and accurately,
Not as the unwise and witless, but wise (sensible,
intelligent people)."

Ephesians 5:15 (AMP)

Your Purpose

In December 2011,
As The Girl Who Lived Between the Hills and the Town
Made preparations for school,
She pondered about her purpose.
She thought of those she knew
Who fearlessly pursued God's purpose and
Briskly walked
To her favorite store;
When she arrived,
The word "Believe"
Greeted her at the doors.

"What makes the word
'Believe'
So unique?"
The response she received three years later
Must have been from
Her Most Gracious Gazillionaire,
Who ignited her heart to believe
And dispelled her fears.

Inventors had to believe!
Those that walked in My purpose believed;
Those who are walking in My purpose believe.
They believe in pursuing their dreams
Using their talents and gifts.

What are your dreams?
What are your talents and gifts?
"All things are possible" My friend!

"Only Believe!"
Watch for doors to My purpose to open.

"Feed My sheep."
That is your purpose.
Use your gifts and talents
To feed those around you;
Express My loving-kindness and mercies to them
As My Son Jesus did for you.

Remember,
"Many are plans in the mind of a man
But it is the purpose of the Lord that will stand."

Your Calling

The Most Gracious Gazillionaire:

    What do you enjoy doing?
    What tasks make you feel at your best?
    Which jobs make you feel at rest
    Peaceful and not stressed?

    What do you enjoy doing?
    What ideas or visions
    Flood your thoughts incessantly?
    Those, My child, are indicating your calling
    And will lead you to My purpose.

    Of course!
    Those activities which make you smile
    And give you satisfaction;
    You are always at your best
    And ready for action.

The Girl Who Lived Between the Hills and the Town:

My calling is lame and makes little money,
I want to dress up and take care of my honey.
I want to travel to Spain;
Chill, sip champagne on a yacht again and again.

The Most Gracious Gazillionaire:

    Who said your calling was too lame?
    Don't harden your heart and complain.
        Think big!
        My child!

My calling is for a reason;
Give it all you've got and stay focused;
Trust me throughout the seasons.

My child, pray about your calling;
Trust Me to lead you
And whatever I say to do,
Do.

When you are at peace,
Elated for being alive,
Working and wanting to do the jive,
That
Is an indication of My calling.
You are happy!
Filled with power!
You work nonstop for many hours.

Appreciate Your Calling

If you run from God's calling,
Then, like Jonah in the Bible
Who found himself in the whale's belly
You and those around you
Will live miserably.

The teaching profession and preaching God's Word
Are callings from which many ran,
Saying they are not as sophisticated
As those of a doctor, lawyer or businessman.

Some parents reject their children
Because their professions do not make them look good;
Not knowing it is the Lord who put the passion
In their children's heart for His purpose
So that they can help others as they should.

Other parents try guiding their children to their calling
Because they recognize the gifts
In them at a very early age;
Giving them their blessings to strengthen those gifts
Without any hindrance or delay.

However, some children
Run away from their calling;
Saying it makes little money;
Keeps them driving in the slow lane
Makes their dressing look crummy.

"A man's gift makes room for him
And brings him before great men."
So appreciate your calling;

It will lead to God's purpose;
Do not abort!
Then live in regret and despair;
Dreaming of what you could have done
If you had trusted Him and not been scared.

Do not be ashamed of your calling.
It is essential for purpose.
Give your all and be diligent.
It will open great doors for you
Make you laugh
And look magnificent!

Appreciate Your Gift

If you compare your gift to others
It could lead you to become jealous;
No gift is more important than the other
Some only require more energy and focus.

"The eye cannot say to the hand
I don't need you!
And the head cannot say to the feet
I don't need you!"
Appreciate your gift
"Do not be anxious..."
See it as a part of your journey to purpose.

Humility – Essential to Walking in Purpose

Humility is essential to walking in purpose.
It is a way of thinking that says,
"Lord, I trust You."
Not saying, "I am unworthy"
As some like to say
And help proudly refuse.

Humility says,
"Lord, though I don't always agree
With my parents, husband, wife,
Pastors, boss or leaders of government,
I will help them to achieve Your purpose;
So, 'Fill them with the knowledge of your will…'
Give them '…the spirit of wisdom
and revelation in the knowledge of Jesus."

"God resist the proud,"
Those who refuse to trust Him;
He "gives grace unto the humble,"
Those who put their faith in Him.
"Humble yourselves therefore under the mighty hands of God…,"
Trust Him to lead you;
"…that He may exalt you in due time"
As purpose finds you.

Walk in Humility;
Don't run away from your purpose.
Appreciate and help God's appointed authorities.
Ask Him to help you respect their positions;
"Having your way"
Can lead to deception.

"Ask and It Shall Be Given"

Why put limits on God?
Why ask for things in doubt
As if He is not able to provide?

We asked,
"Lord, may I have **at least** this?"
We got it.
Ask and believe for more.
He will show us how to get it.

Ask Him to unlock the gifts and talents in you.
"A man's gifts make room for him…"
"Ask, and it shall be given unto you…"
Whatever you ask according to His will,
Believe He hears you
And that the petitions are granted, too.

Go ahead!
Ask Him to unearth all the gifts and talents in you;
Then trust He will lead and
"Direct your path" too.
"Only believe!"
"Don't be afraid!"
"All things are possible!"
Step out in faith!

Exercise Your Faith

A poor image of yourself and your future
Are not of your Heavenly Father.
He put gifts and talents in you to bless you;
Gave you dreams and witty inventions;
But unless you step out and exercise your faith
Then the poor thoughts will consume you
And keep you in detention.

The Lord is the best at all trades
And Master of all;
His talents and gifts
Are in every human to enjoy,
But very few choose to answer the call.

Those who choose to are fearless;
Are not afraid of making mistakes;
They are not shackled
By the works of Old Covenant laws
Or by what people think of them
Or say about their flaws.

When God says, "Move"
They move,
Showing they trust Him as Abraham did.
Abraham believed his Heavenly Father,
Made his mistakes,
Received an abundance of grace
As he exercised his faith.

Trust His Strategy

"My thoughts are not your thoughts
neither are your ways My ways."

In strengthening your gifts and talents
Needed for purpose,
The Lord's way may not
Seem intelligent to the natural mind;
Such as the day Jesus healed a blind man
By placing clay on his eyes.

You may have to resign your job;
Don't hang around **when the Lord** tells you to go;
For it delays the purposes He has for others
Causes setbacks and stops work flow.
When He says, "Submit the letter"
Do as He says and go!

You may have to go to another land
Or be temporarily away from your family;
Don't allow others to discourage you;
The Lord will have your back,
Trust His strategy.

Do what the Lord tells you to do;
He will show you the next step.
Don't run back to the former things
And end up living in regret.

"Abraham never wavered in believing God's promise. In fact, his faith grew stronger, and in this he brought glory to God. He was fully convinced that God is able to do whatever he promises."

Romans 4:20-21 New Living Translation (NLT)

Trusting in "...the Deep"

Trust in the LORD with all thine heart; and lean not unto thine own understanding; In all your ways acknowledge Him, and He shall direct your paths.

Proverbs 3: 5-6

"In God Put Your Trust"

The Girl Who Lived Between the Hills and the Town
Returned to Jamaica in December 2011.
With sponsorship confirmed,
She was granted
An international student visa on January 20, 2012;
Three days later
She picked up the visa from the embassy,
Booked an evening flight
And landed at JFK Airport near midnight.

Coincidentally,
Her passport was stamped January 24, 2012.
Exactly one year since she heard,
"New York is about to come to pass."
She trusted her Heavenly Father
and
Flew directly to New York at last.

Excuse me!
We are from the Pacific
May we have directions to the train?

"In God Put Your Trust."[77]

All the way from Asia we came
How do we get to the Rockaways?

"In God Put Your Trust."

Just landed from Europe

---

[77]Advice based on the U.S. Motto: "In God we trust."

To Manhattan; please…

> *"In God Put Your Trust."*

Africa is our roots
Going to see the Lion King;

> *"In God Put Your Trust."*

We are from Latin and South America
Will be meeting with my family in the Bronx;

> *"In God Put Your Trust."*

Lover of the Caribbean;
Going to Jamaica, Queens; please…

> *"In God Put Your Trust."*

We traveled from the heights and depths
Of the North American lands
How do we get to Long Island and Staten Island?

> *"In God Put Your Trust."*

Please take me to Brooklyn.

> *"In God Put Your Trust."*

"In God Put Your Trust"
What does it really mean?

> It is having confidence
> In The Most High God
> And believing
> He will "Do whatever he promises."

Look at every penny
Every nickel
Every dime
And every dollar
Of this nation;
To be yourself and
Walk in purpose,

"In God Put Your Trust."

They that trust in the LORD shall be as mount Zion, which cannot be removed, but abides forever.

Psalm 125:1 (KJ 2000)

Trusting in "...the Deep" – Part One

The Girl Who Lived Between the Hills and the Town
Launched out into
"...the Deep" of New York City
On her own;
She had no family to be around.

The first seven months in 2012,
Her Heavenly Father opened amazing doors;
Her trust in Him was at its peak;
Well, so she thought until
The trials started and made her weak.

She soon learned to rely on His mercies and grace,
For running back to her island
Would not have allowed her
To finish her race.

The first two semesters
She lived one block from her school;
She felt safe;
To get a cheaper apartment for the next semester,
She would have to dive deeper in faith.

With her new job on campus,
She miraculously got an apartment for September;
She had enough space to praise and dance freely
And neighbours she will always remember.

Fear decided to move in on her job
After the training period ended;
By mid-November
Her confidence went down to a low;
The fear of failure gave her a panic attack;
Oh!
What a blow!

Instead of trusting her Heavenly Father
To work out the situation;
She quit the job on campus
On the day she was given her letter
For "New Hire Orientation."

Later that day,
She was approached by a lady of the Muslim faith
Who handed her a slip of paper with the question,
"Who am I?"
The Girl felt it was to test her faith.

After the conversation with the lady,
The Girl realized she did not know enough
About her identity in Jesus Christ;
The next time she is asked,
"Who am I?"
She would certainly have to get it right.

The Girl Who Lived Between the Hills and the Town
Used the last month of her first year
To read Bible verses on her identity in Christ;
She completed her assignments and baked her fruit cakes;
Forget the recent panic attack that made her body shake.

The Girl understood more about her identity in Christ
As she listened to messages on
The New Covenant in the Bible;
She resumed trusting her Heavenly Father
And launched out to
Meeting new people.

Trusting in "…the Deep" – Part Two

Two ladies offered the Girl accommodation
On the Kings Highway;
She began 2013 in a newly furnished house
At half the price she previously paid.
Though the Girl did not have a job,
She decided to dive deeper in "the Deep"
By trusting her Heavenly Father
For her daily upkeep.

She trusted Him to have her rent and tuition paid
And applied for a permit to work outside
The school's campus;
This permit she hoped
Would not be delayed.

At the beginning of spring,
The Girl had to leave the Kings Highway
Before the rent was due,
Where would she go?
What would she do?

The day before she left
She sat on her suitcases and began to praise,
Received a call the next morning from a friend of a friend
Who surely made her day.

The Girl Who Lived Between the Hills and the Town
Moved from Kings Highway
To Kings Village;
This was close to her school;
There she remained until she graduated;
Wasn't her Heavenly Father cool?

He also moved the church
She was attending
To one block away from her school;
Her Father has a great sense of humor
He does not play the fool.

Her Heavenly Father had her back;
He had made a way;
Yes!
Her Heavenly Father showed her
Mercy, love and care;
How could she not call Him
The Most Gracious Gazillionaire?

At the Kings Village,
The Girl was treated very well;
She got her permit to work part-time outside her school's campus;
She was confident her money issues would be quelled.

She received favor to complete her summer course
And privately tutored for three hours each week;
Started full-time internship in the fall;
There was no time for a twenty-hour job at all.

She trusted her Heavenly Father
Despite the money challenges
And in November,
Received news that her divorce was final,
It was the cherry topping of her trials.

She had a lovely Christmas in New Jersey
With her daughter and friends that year;
Only one semester was left to complete;
By grace, she had completed her second year.

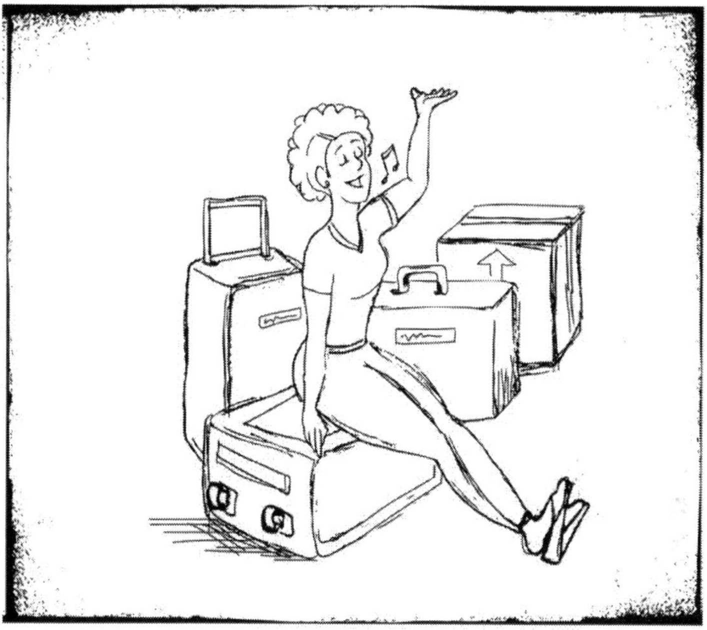

Watch Me Work

The Girl Who Lived Between the Hills and the Town:

It is easy to say have faith
Don't worry
Trust God
Only believe!
Do you know how challenging it is to believe and not see?

      I AM Your Heavenly Father
      The Most Gracious Gazillionaire
      Rich in mercy and tender loving care.
      "Stop Thinking Like a Pauper!"
      Complaining, worrying and walking in fear
      Are not of My nature.
      My "Perfect love casts out all fears"
      Trust me;
      You are in My care.

The Girl Who Lived Between the Hills and the Town:

But that makes no sense;
How can Your love casts out all fears?
How can it increase my faith?
How can it make me less tense?

      At the cross
      My Son Jesus took care of all fears;
      Think on that good news!
      Receive My love!
      Chill;
      Relax;
      No need to run;
      Enjoy yourself!

Go have some fun!

My love is the most powerful, My child;
It is not something for which you work;
Receive My love as a gift and be thankful;
Trust Me,
Watch Me work.

SIMONE A. CLARKE

Fear or Faith

Fear or Faith
Which will you choose?
Choose fear
You will lose;
Choose faith
Your patience with be tested;
But "All things will work together for good
to them that love God..."
For in Him they have rested.

Fear will make you anxious
Remove your peace and
Make you obnoxious;
It will lead to stress;
Cause you to become ill;
Rob you of rest
Which is not God's will.

Fear is a trap to hinder you;
It is the twin brother of worry;
A trap for you to keep the "Status quo"
"Better to be safe than to be sorry."

Staying safe is good;
But it has side effects, too;
It can remove faith needed for inventions,
Hinder production and keep you feeling blue.

How do you feel
When you make a promise to someone
And you are not trusted?
Or you find out that the one you love doubts you?
How do you think the Lord feels

When He is not trusted?
He is "not slack concerning" His promises.

Those who have faith in Him
Are the ones who will always please Him;
The man who walks in fear
Has "…little faith…" in Him.

Which will you choose?
Fear or Faith?
Choose wisely;
You determine the life you create.

Seasons

"There is a season for everything" under the sun.
A time to cry, a time to have fun;
A time when your life seems to be standing still
And another time you're always on the run.

Fall and winter are the dampest times
The time when there seems to be no hope;
Some hibernate
Cut themselves off from others;
Others die for they are unable to cope.

Then there are those who stay
In faith and believe
And thus endure the winter bummer;
They are the ones
Who trust during those cold seasons
And harvest greatly in the springtime and summer.

Oh, what a joy!
They have in the warm seasons
As they reap the fruits of their faith;
They trusted and
Stayed positive;
Hoped and relied on God's Grace.

The Cup on the Window Sill

How long
Should I endure these tasks
Which keep me daily in the books?
I have been studying, studying, studying
With very little time to cook.

"You don't have to do this,"
The devil whispers;
"You have lots of time…;
Put it off for another year
You prefer living on a dime?"

But I'm no movie star or singer
Who make thousands within a year;
I've got to beat the books
So I can go earn my fair share.

"No, you don't have to!
That is a big lie!
All you need is a partner with money
Who promises love that won't die."

   Back to earth, My child!
  This is Your Most Gracious Gazillionaire;
   The cup on the window sill
   Is to remind you I AM here.

  Read the cup on the window sill;
   "Don't quit" it reads;
    Don't quit
    Don't quit
    Don't quit!
   Finish your studies;
    Be encouraged;
    Don't quit.

SIMONE A. CLARKE

This is Only Temporary

The Most Gracious Gazillionaire:

> So you feel you have waited long enough
> To walk in the purpose for which you were created?
> Just a little longer, My child
> Your wait is only temporary.

The Girl Who Lived Between the Hills and the Town:

"Temporary?
How long is temporary?
I have been waiting for months!"

The Most Gracious Gazillionaire:

> To walk in your purpose
> You will be tested;
> Sometimes scorned or even rejected;
> Though the process seems long
> Seems like a tussle,
> It will work your patience
> And build your muscles.
>
> Temporary could be a thousand,[8]
> Four hundred or forty years;
> Seven years or even twelve months;
> Twenty-four hours;
> Three days;
> Forty days or seven months.

---

[8] See Notes under title "This Is Only Temporary".

"Temporary," My child
Will also depend on you;
Just cooperate with the process
And watch it expire soon.

Pruning

Not because we have not yet seen
The things for which we ask,
Means our Heavenly Father does not love us.
We may be in the process of maturing
Or maybe we are just being pruned.

Now pruning should not be resented;
It is necessary
For the purpose
Our Heavenly Father intended;
To bear much fruit both inside and out
So that you can impact others
Without casting doubts.

So when He says,
"I AM pruning you."
Trust Him!
It is preparation
For the purpose
He has for you.

Refining

Jesus is like a
"Refiner's fire."
In Him our spirit, soul and body are refined;
Refined "As gold and silver."

His process of refining
Began at the cross;
There He took our curses, judgment, shame and sins;
Our spirit is refined and made like His
The moment we accept and believe in Him.

Now your soul
Is being refined
Especially during times of stress;
The aim is to build your trust in God
By keeping your mind, will and emotions
At rest.

Refine your body
With proper rest and exercise;
Drink plenty water;
Eat balanced meals;
If you ignore refining your body,
It will weaken the soul
And make you reel.

Do not get discouraged
When you are being refined;
Remain in an atmosphere
Of trusting, thankfulness and praise;
Renew your mind in God's Word,
Pray and "Be still!"
Know that "The Lord of Hosts is thy God"
And has given you His grace.

Be Faithful

Be committed
To what you were called to do.
Focus.
Others are waiting on you
To pass on the baton
So they can run, too.

Be faithful
Despite how hard things get;
Don't quit!
The Father is not
Done with you yet.

Finish Strong!

Why procrastinate
On that task you were given?
You have been putting it off for weeks;
Get off your rump!
Go work at it now!
Dwelling on the past will make you weak!

Finish strong!
Stop looking back!
Unfinished work is waiting on you;
Finish strong!
Stop looking back!
Other doors are waiting
To be opened for you.

Trusting in "the Deep" – Finale

The Girl Who Lived Between the Hills and the Town
Began her final semester January 2014;
How would she pay her expenses?
She had three tutoring jobs by March;
Worked the twenty hours permitted;
Received grad waivers, scholarships, refunds
And a stipend for volunteer work;
June 2014, she graduated.

July she had
Fifteen hundred dollars in arrears for tuition;
Had she trusted her Heavenly Father
And spent that amount wisely the previous semester,
Her balance would have been zero
On the school's register.

Studying in New York City
Made her appreciate
"The day of small things,"
For though you will have trials and testing,
The Almighty God
"Will never leave you,"
In Him,
Keep on trusting.

Trust = Faith + Action

The Girl Who Lived Between the Hills and the Town
Launched out into "the Deep,"
Despite the many distractions;
And now confirms:
Trust = Faith + Action.

Trust = Faith + Action
This formula is easy to memorize;
Many have used it
Made their mistakes
Grown
And become very wise.

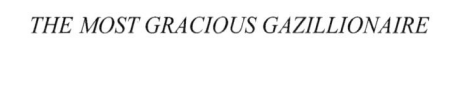

"**Even so faith, if it has not works, is dead, being alone.**"

James 2:17 (KJ 2000)

The Girl Who Lived Between the Hills and the Town is Thankful

**In everything give thanks:
for this is the will of God in Christ Jesus
concerning you.**

2 Thessalonians 3:4

Weathering "...the Deep" – Coat Weight

When The Girl Who Lived Between the Hills and the Town
"Launched out into the deep,"
A friend cautioned,
"Be prepared for a bitter winter."
A miracle however took place that semester;
There was no snow or cold to fear
It was a welcomed start to her school year.

But on that day in the fall
Her first walk in snow,
A comedy show
She put on
As she tiptoed
In heeled boots
On the road to her home.

The coats got thicker
In the second winter;
Thank God for another friend
Who warned,
"This year you will experience the real thing."
My! Oh! My!
If the Girl had known
She would have bought five pairs of gloves!
The two pairs she wore were sure not enough.

Finally!
Summer came;
The Girl was so delighted;
A classmate said to her,
"I did not know you were so small!"
The thick coats and sweaters
Had deceived her classmate during the winter;
She was able to shed
The coat weight in the summer.

Weathering "...the Deep" – Butt of a Joke

After being told
It would be "Very nippy"
In the fall of her second year;
"The Girl Who Lived Between the Hills and the Town"
Overdressed in October
And was the butt of a joke
On a bus ride to remember.

As she sat on a NYC transit bus,
Two men speaking
The Jamaican Patois said loudly,
"Taaap! A Winta!"[9]
They assumed the Girl
Would not understand their language;
She turned around in her seat
And to them said boldly,
"Mi kaan deal wid di cole."[10]
The other passengers started laughing;
She joined in with them
And almost started coughing.

On her last day of winter in the big city
The Girl's phone said temperature
Would be in the sixties;
She dressed in orange and white
Welcoming the colors of the new season;
Fitted heeled boots as a fashion statement
Well, that was her reason.

---

[9] "It seems as if it is winter!" (hinting it is fall and the Girl was dressed for winter)
[10] "The weather is too cold for me"

Surprise! Surprise!
To her dismay it snowed;
She had misread her phone
Or maybe she needed a new phone;
What to do but to laugh at herself
And play in the snow on her way home.

Thanksgiving Day

To my friends and family in the United States
Have a great Thanksgiving Day
To the others around the world
Give thanks for another day.

Thanksgiving Dinner

Roasted Turkey Wings and Cranberry Sauce
Collard Greens and Cornbread
Candied Potatoes, Sweet and Sour Meatballs, Green
Garden Salad
Oh! What a spread!
Jamaican Rice and Peas with Fried Breadfruit,
Ice Cream and Apple Pie
A lovely New York City Thanksgiving
I am stuffed and ready to fly.

Thank You

For waking me, Lord
I thank You.
For Your gift of righteousness
I thank You.
For peace and joy
I thank You.
For rest
I thank You, too.

Lord, We Give You Thanks

Lord, we give You thanks for everything;
Oceans that teach dolphins to sing as enchanted kings;
Big bright blue skies that climb high
When we try to get nigh;
They give us food and water as a mother nurturing.

Christmas is Here!

Mr. Word confidently sang to Mr. Doubt about his Heavenly Father's love:

Christmas has come;
Chicken is in the pot;
Seasoned with onion,
Hot red and yellow "scotch"[11]
If you have nothing to give
A smile will do;
If you don't have a smile
Remember…
The Father loves you.

Mr. Doubt responded:

I hear you!
Christmas is here.
Chicken is in your pot.
The Father loves me?
Really? (Sarcastically)
What has The Father done for me lately?

Mr. Word answered:

Well, He sent His "Only begotten Son" Jesus
Who was rejected so that you can be accepted.

His son took wounding for your transgressions
And bruises for your iniquities

---

[11]Scotch bonnet peppers

So that you would be free from sin and condemnation
And be delivered from the sins of your former generations.
He took chastisement so that you could have peace;
Took stripes on His body so that you can be healed.

At the cross Jesus was naked;
He had no shelter,
He hungered and thirsted;
So that you can now have clothing and shelter
Never hunger nor thirst.

Though Jesus "Was rich,
Yet for your sakes he became poor
That you through his poverty might be rich."

Jesus hung on that cross
And became a curse for you;
So that you would be redeemed
"From the curse of the law"
"That the blessing of Abraham might come on" you.

Your Father made Jesus "who knew no sin"
To be sin for you;
That you
"Might be made the righteousness of God in Him."

Mr. Doubt took Mr. Word's words as seeds in his heart. He allowed no persecution or trial to destroy them; Allowed no thorns of deceit or strife to choke them. He watered those seeds, gave them light, meditated on them and within a year he began growing strong roots and bearing fruits. While at the shopping mall the following Christmas, Mr. Doubt who had changed his name to Mr. Faith, spotted Mr. Word and shouted to him:

Christmas is here!
Jesus Christ has redeemed me!
In Him, I am "Set free from sin";
"Blessed are those whose lawless deeds are forgiven
and whose sins are covered;
Blessed is the man to whom the Lord shall not impute sin."

As the people in the mall stopped to listen, Mr. Faith shouted:

This Christmas
Bless the Lord!
"And forget not all His benefits"!
He "forgives all your iniquities"
"Heals all your diseases"
"Redeems your life from destruction"
"Crowns you with loving-kindness and tender mercies"
"Satisfies your mouth with good things
so that your youth is renewed like the eagle's."

In Christ Jesus you have
"Redemption through His blood,
the forgiveness of sins, according to the
riches of His grace…"

You are a new creature in Christ;
You are "Accepted in" Christ;
You are seated in "Heavenly places in Christ."

You are "Complete in" Christ.
You are "More than a conqueror" in Christ.
You "Can do all things through Christ"
Because you "Have the mind of Christ."

In Christ you are redeemed
"From the curse of the law"
Over you "Sin shall not have dominion."
You are "Under grace"
You are blessed!
You are redeemed from condemnation,
Sickness, poverty and destruction;
He died for you
And "...was raised again for your justification."

Mr. Faith rejoiced and sang:
"O come let us adore Him;
O come let us adore Him;
O come let us adore Him;
Christ the Lord!" [12]
Only believe!
Receive your Heavenly Father's love
As your Christmas gift!
Because of His son's obedience
Many shall "Be made righteous."

So whenever the thought comes
"What has the Heavenly Father done for me lately?"
Remember:
He brought Christmas
Through His Son Jesus.

---

[12] Taken from the hymn "O Come, All Ye Faithful" by John Francis Wade.

Happy New Year – Write the Vision

I am Your Heavenly Father,
The Most Gracious Gazillionaire.
Happy New Year!
Write the visions and the plans;
Draw them if you can.
Put in a place where you will always see them
And pray about them.

If you are unable to see, write or draw
Ask for help
And make use of technology;
Ask Me to show you how to make the vision a reality.
Record everything which comes in your heart
Trusting I will provide the resources
And show you how to start.

You will have a great year walking in My purpose;
Just be yourself
And don't lose focus.
"My grace is sufficient for you,"
Was how you lived last year;
That same "Grace is sufficient"
For you to go through another year.

Happy Birthday – Smile!

You are getting older
But have not yet achieved your dream;
What are you waiting for?
Get up and celebrate!
Go celebrate that dream!

Keep focused
Because distractions will come;
Don't be afraid
To politely say,
"May I be excused?
I have a goal to work on."

Happy birthday!
Smile!
For it looks good on you
Smile!
Your dreams will come through soon.

Friends

Thirty years of friendship
We have come a long way!
What a blessing you have been
For journeying with me throughout the years.
You had my back when I faced the crowd
And the competition became fierce;
During the challenges of the reign
You were my eyes when mine had tears.

When the loss came
You gave your support with witty words
And put things in perspective
When I was heading to the rum bar to curse.
You believed in my calling
And for that I am forever grateful;
Thank you for being my friend
You are a forever treasure to the end.

To my other friend of twenty two years:
We travelled on those faraway trips;
Cooking curry chicken and cartwheel dumplings;[13]
Eating seafood and potato chips;
I thank you for your patience
And all your support
For during our heated discussions
You did not run or quit.

To those friends who spoke frankly
Thank you so much for your honesty;
To those who understand what stress is
Thank you for putting laughter in the mix.

---

[13] Flour dough shaped like wheels of four to six inches in diameter, then boiled in water.

To the seasonal and permanent friends
And those on the favorite social websites:
Thank you;
I love you;
Hope your day will be cheerful and bright.

Grateful to the Men

The Girl Who Lived Between the Hills and the Town
Expresses sincere gratitude
To all the people who helped her
To begin her journey to purpose.

On the first day she arrived in the Big Apple
She met Chris;
His name reminded her
To follow after Christ Jesus.

On the second day
She was introduced to Joshua,
The Hebrew name for Jesus;
To remind her Jesus is
The only God who is able to save;
He is her salvation
And her redemption.

Within the third month there was Daniel
To remind her that God is her judge
And would keep her throughout the fiery trials;
He is not a judge who condemns,
But the judge who sent his Son Jesus to take all her judgements
So that she could live freely from condemnation
During the trials and temptations.

Then there was Benjamin,
Which means "son of the right hand";
He was sent in time to remind the girl that
Jesus is "The Son of man" at God's right hand
And that she is "The righteousness of God in him."

As the Girl approached her final year of school
Emmanuel came
To share things she needed to know
And to remind her God was with her
And would not let her go.

When the graduation passed
And not yet seeing a full-time job,
He sent Michael to remind her,
"Who is like God?"
Then the little angel Gabriel came
To remind her that God is her Strength and
That she was able to write this book of poetry
"Through Christ who strengthens" her.

When the first draft of the book was written,
He sent Isaac
Whose name reminded her to
Laugh, laugh, laugh;
For by the grace of God
She accomplished a task;
He made the impossible possible
Made her laugh, laugh, laugh.

Five days before sending this book to the next stage
She met David.
His name reminded her
To be conscious of Jesus and His Father's love;
For no matter our status, color, ethnicity or gender
We are His and are dearly loved.

And did she meet Joseph?
Yes, she did!
She met two Josephs;
One had the first name Joseph
The other's last name was Joseph;

They reminded her to always,
"Be Like Joseph."[14]

The name Joseph means "Jehovah increases"
Or "He will add."
Through Jehovah's Son, Jesus
Limitless grace and mercies
Were given to us.

---

[14] See the poems "Be Like Joseph" in Volume Two

Grateful to the Ladies

The Girl Who Lived Between the Hills and the Town
Expresses sincere gratitude to nine ladies
Who reminded her
Of "The fruit of the Spirit"
As she swam in "The Deep" of New York City.

While on the "King's Highway"
Two ladies taught her to maintain her *faith* and *joy*
For those fruits were needed to maintain her energy
Which in the storms she had to employ.

Then she met three widows and three sisters
Who showed her "*Love, patience, kindness,
Goodness, faithfulness, gentleness* and *self-control*;"
Just like the widow who cared for Elijah,
They treated her like royalty in their villas.

The ninth lady
Reminded the Girl weekly to
"Be at peace"
For
"God will keep in perfect peace
Those whose minds are steadfast,
Because they trust in Him."

Grateful to All

There were many more people
Who helped the Girl along the way,
Such as those who visited from the island
Who always "made her day."

God knows you will need to have friends with whom to relax;
Friends to pray with, visit places, eat with and just chat.
Those were the times the Girl was extremely grateful;
For being in a city without an immediate family,
Sometimes made her tearful.

The Girl acknowledges the people
Who helped her from the start;
Her parents, relatives, and friends of many years
Who called and blessed her heart.

To her brave and gracious daughter
She says, "Thank you!
For adjusting; making yourself happy;
Staying focused and being you."

To all who cared for her daughter
The Girl says,
"Thank you;
'For we know that all things work together for
 good to them that love God, to them who are the
called according to his purpose.'"

Be Yourself and Walk in Purpose

"Without counsel purposes are disappointed: but in the multitude of counselors they are established."

Proverbs 15:22

Your Name and Purpose

Abram to Abraham
Sarai to Sarah
Jacob to Israel
Simon to Peter
Saul to Paul.

In the Bible
Their names were changed
To fit God's calling and purpose.

What is your name?
What is your calling?
Be yourself
Walk in His purpose.

Rare Diamond

You are a hidden treasure
A rare diamond indeed!
Don't be foolish in letting others
Talk you out of God's plans,
He "will supply your need."

Do not concern yourself
With what others think of you.
They criticized Jesus
They will do the same to you.

As a rare diamond
Be resilient!
You are seated in
"The Rock"!
You are magnificent!

We Are SPECIAL

Tics, Tics, Tics,
It is called Tourette Syndrome;[15]
Every three minutes we stretch our necks
And show off our tongues;
Sometimes we sniff, blink frequently;
Bark or speak inappropriately.

Some say we are not too bright
We get tantrums and start fights;
Not many want to be our friends
ADHD we have
How we wish it would end.

She can speak from a platform
And not be nervous;
Yet to interact in small social settings
She becomes very anxious.

He does not like others hugging him;
Just give him a high five;
Loud noise and bells are not his taste;
He will cover his ears or become irate.

"Go get the other kids with "burgers"
Commanded the new teacher at our school;
Had she known about "Asperger's."
She would not have made us feel like fools.

---

[15]For an explanation of this and other underlined terms used in this poem, refer to the Glossary.

Our condition is termed <u>Down's Syndrome;</u>
We are one of the most sociable people on earth;
We have calling and purpose
That is why we were birthed.

There are so many disorders
And disabilities in this world;
Some call us "disabled,"
Others "retarded" and "nerds."
If only they understood
How smart and loving we really are;
We call ourselves SPECIAL
Yes!
SPECIAL we are.

We thank You, Lord
You have never left us;
We were born
For a special purpose;
We are SPECIAL!
Yes!
SPECIAL we are.
We are SPECIAL!
Do you know who you are?

I Am Loved

Are you intimidated by those who ask,
Who are you?

Don't be afraid!
Be yourself!

Speak boldly and respond,
"I am loved by the I AM."

I am a father;
I am loved by the I AM.
I work and provide for my children;
I affirm,
Express my love,
Hug and encourage them;
I am honest, considerate, wise and strong,
When I make mistakes, I apologize
And let them know I was wrong.

I am a mother;
I am loved by the I AM.
I am caring, encouraging, pleasant and nurturing;
I am patient, courageous, humble and loving;
I am wise, I plan and organize;
I ensure my children eat healthily;
And speak life over them
That they may think wealthily.

I am a husband;
I am loved by the I AM.
I am faithful and forgiving;
I love my wife very much;
I am kind;

I give to her;
She melts under my touch.
When she speaks I listen;
Her eyes shine and glisten;
I am happy to take her out
And let my friends see her without a doubt.

I am a wife;
I am loved by the I AM.
I am down-to-earth, capable
Cheerful and affectionate;
I am intelligent, forgiving
Reliable and considerate;
I am sincere, unselfish,
Knowledgeable and tactful;
I dress well and look great!
I've got my husband's back
And I'm helpful.

I am neither a mother nor a wife;
But I love who I am.
I am loved by the I AM.
I am a responsible, emotionally stable
And virtuous woman
Who "reigns in life"
Without fear, stress and condemnation.

I am neither a father nor a husband
But I love who I am;
I am loved by the I AM.
I am responsible and kind;
A disciplined man
Who "reigns in life"
Without fear, stress and condemnation.

Whether you are a boy or girl, woman or man

Be yourself.
Know who you are.
You are loved by
Your Heavenly Father above.
His Son Jesus
Took your punishment
So that you would not
Receive His judgement.

So next time you are asked,
"Who are you?"
Please respond,
"I am loved;
Loved by the great, great, great
"I AM."

Jesus a Mi Friend*   Jesus is My Friend
(Dub poem)

Jesus, Never leave mi, Even when mi friends forsake mi, A Him alone receive mi, When the people out a road ill-treat mi.	Jesus, Will never leave me; Should my friends forsake me; He alone receives me When all others ill-treat me.
Chorus Jesus a mi fren Jesus a mi fren His luv will neva end His luv will neva end; Jesus a mi fren Jesus a mi fren His luv will neva end His luv will neva end.	**Chorus** Jesus is my friend Jesus is my friend His love will never end His love will never end; Jesus is my friend Jesus is my friend His love will never end His love will never end.

I am
Royalty;
My Father is
The Gazillionaire King
His righteous robe I wear and sing;
He loves me
Will not make me ashamed
I receive His love, mercy and grace.
(Repeat Chorus in Patois then English)

---

* Jamaican Creole (patois)

Be Yourself and Walk in Purpose

Diversity is God's nature.
Each of you has unique fingerprints
So not to be like others
But to be yourself
Using your talents and gifts.
Do not be ashamed!
Be yourself!
Walk in purpose
Without fear or guilt!

Be yourself!
Walk in purpose!
Storms will come
But in God put your trust.
Don't be afraid!
The "battle is not yours" to fight.
The Lord will be your defense
Go!
Reach for new heights.

Bi Tankful for Woo Yu Bi
Jamaican Patois

The Most Gracious Gazillionaire Speaks:

You hav ball head?
Yu waan long hair?
Since yu brain good
And you no mad
Be creeativ wid what yu have
And be tankful.

The Insecure:

Mi eyes dem big
Eaz look like satellite
Nose look like a pig;
Lips thin like wafa
Mi wish mi coulda sing
And do a gig.

The Most Gracious Gazillionaire:

Yu can see, ear an smell,
Chat, nyam and swallow yu bread?
Be tankful

Be Thankful for Who You Are
English Translation

The Most Gracious Gazillionaire Speaks:

Are you bald-headed?
Do you wish you had long hair?
Since your brain is intact
and you are of sound mind
Be creative with what you have
And be thankful.

The Insecure:

My eyes are so big
Ears are like satellite
Nose resembles one of a pig;
Lips are as thin as a wafer
If only I could sing
And do a gig.

The Most Gracious Gazillionaire:

Can you see, hear and smell,
Speak, eat, and swallow your bread?
Be thankful.

The Insecure:

Mi neck long like galin;
Mi chest flat like pancake;
Mi belly big, big, big;
Mi wear belly ban all di time fi look slim.

The Most Gracious Gazillionaire:

Yu can breede?
Yu have yu heart, lungs and kidneys?
Yu belly full?
Be tankful.

The man who believes God has not heard his prayers:

Mi wish mi coulda get mi wife pregnant.
She waan nuff pickney
Fi tek care a.

The Most Gracious Gazillionaire:

Yu tek care a pickney whey nuh have nuh parents;
Yu mek odder people pickney feel so special;
Dem love yu nuff nuff.
Dem wish them own muma and pupa never

The Insecure:

My neck is as long as an egret's;
My chest is flat like a pancake;
My tummy is so large;
Every day I wear a corset.

The Most Gracious Gazillionaire:

Can you breathe freely?
Are your heart, lungs and kidneys in place?
Is your stomach full?
Be thankful.

The man who believes God has not heard his prayers:

It is my wife I wish to impregnate;
She wants to conceive, give birth, nurture and generate.

The Most Gracious Gazillionaire

You raised orphans;
You make the children of others feel accepted;
They appreciate you so much;
Wishing their own parents did not make them feel rejected.
You make a difference in their

mek dem feel like dem a nuh smady.
Yu do a lot fi dem;
Be tankful.

lives;
Be thankful.

The Insecure:

Mi legs dem maga and long, long long;
Mi wear size 14 shoes
Wid long long toes like King Kong.

The Insecure:

My legs are thin and very long;
I wear size 14 shoes
With very long toes like King Kong.

The Most Gracious Gazillionaire:

Yu can walk, run, hop, skip, jump, dance and kick?
Be tankful.

The Most Gracious Gazillionaire:

Can you walk, run, hop, skip, jump, dance and kick?
Be thankful.

The enemy speaks:

"Look pon dem skin;
Fi him white and ugly like duppy;
Fi har spreckle like banana;
And fi dem blac like bun up bread."

The enemy speaks:

"Look at their skin;
His skin is as white as a ghost;
Her skin is as freckled as a banana
Their skin are as dark as burnt toast."

The Insecure now Confident:

A ina di sun yu waa mi fi go get color pan mi white skin fi please yu?

The Insecure now Confident:

Should I get a tan to please you?
I love my freckles

Mi love mi spreckles
and mi know dem cute.

Wi nah go bleach
Wi blac skin
Fi get yu fi like wi;
Yu bias show sey yu
dunce and fraid a wi.

So since yu have a
problem wid wi skin
Know dis,

Wi skin protect wi bodi
tissue and organs;
Wi skin keep dem
warm;
Wi Alive!
Wi rich, rich rich Fada
Gad
luv wi!
We luv who wi is!
"Wi fearfully and
wonderfully made..."
Wi tankful!

Only "By di grace a
Gad
I am what I am."
Only "By di grace a
Gad"
Can wi be wiself and
walk in Fada Gad
purpose.

Laud,
We tank Yu
Fi meking us.

and know they are cute.

No bleaching for these "burnt toast"
skin
To get you to accept us;
Your prejudices are revealing
Your ignorance and fear of us.

If you have a problem with our skin
Consider this,

Our body tissues and organs are
protected by our skin;
They are kept warm by our skin;
We are alive!
Our Gazillionaire Father loves us!
We love who we are!
We are "fearfully
And wonderfully made..."
We are thankful!

Only "By the grace of God
I am what I am."
Only "By the grace of God"
Can we be ourselves and walk in
His purpose.

Lord,
We thank You
For creating us.

Thank you for making me so wonderfully complex!
Your workmanship is marvelous—how well I know it.
You watched me as I was being formed in utter
seclusion,
as I was woven together in the dark of the womb.
You saw me before I was born.
Every day of my life was recorded in your book.
Every moment was laid out
before a single day had passed. How precious are your
thoughts about me, O God.
They cannot be numbered!
I can't even count them;
they outnumber the grains of sand!
And when I wake up,
you are still with me!

Psalm 139:14-18 NLT

Take Me Out of Your Box

I Am your Heavenly Father,
The Most Gracious Gazillionaire.
I choose "the foolish things of this world
to confound the wise."
So take me out of your box
For I AM Limitless.

Because you studied to be a teacher
Does not mean you cannot own a yacht.
If you dropped out of school
You can be a CEO, too.
If you are now a housekeeper,
It does not mean you
Will always be using sweepers.

Don't be afraid to serve.
Draw, paint, sing,
Babysit, counsel, teach the kids;
Write the poems, songs, movies and books,
Clean the floor,
Farm and cook.

"Whatever your hands find to do
Do it with thy might…"
"Do it heartily, as to the Lord, and not unto men."
For the knowledge gained
Is a part of your journey to purpose;
Trust Me
No need to feel ashamed or nervous.

If you find yourself feeling stressed,
That is not My will;

Choose to "enter into My rest,"
Rest which comes by trusting Me
Rest and be still.

Watch Me cause
All things to "work together for good
to them that love God…"
And those who come in your path will benefit;
Benefit from your talents and gifts
Walk in their purpose and remove their deficits.

Don't allow others' expectation of you
To dictate what you do.
The past has gone and cannot be relived;
Trust Me
Believe Me
You have much in you to give.

I Am your Heavenly Father
The Most Gracious Gazillionaire;
Is anything too hard for Me to do?
"The silver is Mine and the gold is Mine."
"Every beast of the forest is Mine."
The "cattle on a thousand hills" are Mine.
Everything in this world has a purpose;
And like the bees, rivers and trees
You
Can walk in your calling and purpose.

As Jesus is bold
So are you "in this world."
"Do not be afraid,
Only believe"!
Step out in faith!
"Launch out into the deep"!

Diving Deeper in "...the Deep" – Part One

After graduation,
The Girl Who Lived Between the Hills and the Town
Decided to remain in New York City;
She thought it best to earn some money
Before returning to her country.

She moved from Kings Village in Brooklyn
To the borough of Queens;
She rested that summer;
Trusting her Heavenly Father for her needs.

The Girl had her new work permit
And T.A. certification by the end of September;[16]
But another panic attack the night before a job presentation,
Was the trigger for job rejections in October.

She cried to her Heavenly Father
For help in November;
He prompted her to write;
But instead of chronicling as she normally would,
Poetry flowed from her pen that night.

After writing forty poems within three weeks,
She heard, "This is a new assignment for purpose."
Two days after Christmas
Her Heavenly Father spoke again,
"Be Yourself and Walk in Purpose."

The Girl Who Lived Between the Hills and the Town
Was not aware of pent-up anger until writing her poems;
Was there a connection between the anger in her veins

---

[16]T.A. – Teaching Assistant

And the two-centimeter lump she found in her right breast?
February 2015, there were many questions;
Was this the beginning of another test?

She was prompted to write on forgiveness and healing;
She wrote and refined the poems "Be Like Joseph."
The lump, which her doctor confirmed was a cyst,
Disappeared by mid-April
It surely was not missed.

Thanks to her Heavenly Father,
The one rich in grace, mercy and care,
How could she not call Him
The Most Gracious Gazillionaire?

Diving Deeper in "...the Deep" – Part Two

The Girl Who Lived Between the Hills and the Town
Tutored and wrote over a hundred poems in five months.
When the Common Core exams were over,
She finally left New York City
And headed down south
To Palm Beach County.

As her manuscripts were edited
She met new friends in therapy;
Her Heavenly Father provided
A "Divorce Care" group,
To help with the negative emotions
That had taken root.

When her therapy was over,
She spent a few weeks at a creek in Georgia;
It had a name which meant
"Jehovah has been gracious,"
Her Heavenly Father confirmed that
She was in His purpose.

At last!
The editing of her manuscripts was finally complete;
She returned to her country August 2015
Finally,
She was now out of "...The Deep"!

But her Heavenly Father explained,
"...The Deep" is a way of thinking
That puts its trust in God;
A mindset of going into the unknown by faith
And believing the Lord is with you despite the wait.

"...The Deep"
Was not just New York City, Florida or Georgia;
It also included her country, Jamaica.
More poems were downloaded in her heart in September,
She returned to the United States in the month of October.

The Girl spent hours in the Bible,
Researched scriptures related to her poems;
Edited texts and adjusted titles.

The Girl's family thought she had become a recluse;
But she needed this time alone to finish her new task;
For she knew in her heart
The time would soon pass.

In January 2016
She departed from Florida,
Returned to her country,
The island of Jamaica.

Diving Deeper in "...the Deep" – Part Three

2006 – 2018
The Girl Who Lived Between the Hills and the Town
Had her worlds shaken.
Her ideal world of "married for over forty years as parents,
Grandparents and great grandparents" was broken.
Her world of "Mother will live for over eighty years as her
parents and grandparents" stolen.

Leaving the security of a permanent job with benefits
To go and study in New York City
Built the Girl's faith,
"The Lord shall provide all my needs…"
Is what she now states.

When there was no more car,
He provided train, bus or "dollar cab."
When she could not pay her rent
Tutoring jobs he sent.

When her students said
Her clothes were looking old;
In her mind she knew
She was not naked or cold.

When comments were made
That she was skinny,
The doctor confirmed that she was healthy.

Who said the Girl's life
Did not show God's grace?
In the little or much,
There is always sufficient grace.

You may have planned your future
But you were detoured;
How the change is handled
Could leave you floored.

You may be angry your life did not
Turn out the way you had planned;
Admit your anger
As you speak with your Heavenly Father.
Begin to appreciate,
"The exceeding riches of his grace."
Receive His love, mercy and care,
You will see why He is called
The Most Gracious Gazillionaire.

August 2018,
Seven years after the Girl *did*
"Submit the Letter…"
She was confident life could only get better.
This was confirmed after an almost
Two and a half years' wait for her correct salary;
She now awaits to answer the question
Did the Girl ever remarry?

Diving Deeper in "…the Deep" – Finale

The Girl Who Lived Between the Hills and the Town
Received her Heavenly Father's
Gift of Salvation at age nineteen;
But soon after, did things her way;
She had no knowledge about purpose.

Four years later
She compiled a worship song book
With hymns and other popular songs for her church
Not knowing Her Heavenly Father
Was guiding her to purpose.

Eleven years after,
The Girl wrote her first drama script and song
For her trainees to perform at devotion at work;
Still unaware that ministering to others
Using the performing arts was birthed.

In 2012, when she launched "Out into the Deep"
To study in "The City That Never Sleeps",
Writing her own book was not on her mind then
But in her first week of studies,
One of her assignments was to create
A math story book for children.

She requested twice to do field work at the
Elementary school which majors in mathematics;
She was rejected;
Ironically,
By their neighbour who majors in the performing arts,
She was accepted.

She used song in a presentation on fractions;
Her professor and classmates received with satisfaction.
She used poetry and song in her math story book;
She had done it!
Written her first book.

The Girl began expressing her emotions
In poetry, November 2014;
Then a desire to write poetry on,
"The Gospel of the Grace of God"
Became her new focus;
She would use the poems
To "**Feed My Sheep**."
The Most Gracious Gazillionaire
Brought her to His purpose.

He brought her back to her country
The place she had begun;
But this time she no longer
Lived Between the Hills and the Town;
Only on "The Plain"
Which she calls home.

You may have various talents and gifts
And feel confused about your calling and purpose;
Ask the Lord,
"What do you want me to do?"
He will guide you to **His** calling and purpose.

Going to school?
Getting married?
Starting a business or changing a career?
To walk into God's purpose
Trust Him to guide you!
Give no attention to fear!

A Pleasant Administrator and Team Leader

"Mi teecha pregnant again![17]
But she jus ave baby the oder day!
Mi a go call ar di 'Mats and Litricha Pregnant Teecha.'
Ar pickney dem a go bi teecha;
One a go teech Mats and di oder Drama."

        Ivy Elizabeth Lynch Clarke
        Served 1976 -1979 as a
        Mathematics and Literature teacher
        At Oberlin High School,
        St. Andrew, Jamaica.

She left Oberlin High 1979 to teach at her Alma mater
        St. Mary's College;
        A Catholic high school
Nestled above and within the rocks of St. Catherine.
She ascended and descended at least 100 steps daily
        Led the Mathematics department
        And had another baby.

     Mrs. Clarke worked as Grade Coordinator
     Then as Vice Principal;
     Served St. Mary's College for 28 years,
     Then returned to Oberlin High in 2007
     Where she retired in 2015
     After serving as Principal for eight years.

---

[17] This stanza is written in Jamaican creole.
Translation in English - "My teacher is pregnant again! But she recently had a baby! I will call her the 'Math and Literature Pregnant Teacher.' Her children will be teachers; One with teach Math and the other Drama."

On her return to Oberlin High
Thoughts of how much the school had grown
Was foremost in her mind;
"How will I fill the shoes
Of my predecessors?"
She asked.
They are legends;
One of a kind.

For eight years
Mrs Clarke traversed Oberlin's mountains
Though very steep to climb;
She put her trust in the Almighty God
And wore a broad smile.

Her passion for music never left her soul;
The traditions of the Oberlin Choir
She did uphold;
Mrs. Clarke continued the traditions of
Leading the Eastern Championship,
4H and cheerleading teams;
The Oberlin farm and hospitality department
Would always make her beam.

Ivy Elizabeth Lynch Clarke
Wuz ere![18]
A dedicated, warm-hearted and generous teacher;
Served at Oberlin High School for 11 years,
Not only as the "Mats and Litricha Pregnant Teecha"
But as an avid supporter
Of the Arts, Science, Technology, Business and Sports;
A pleasant administrator and team leader.

---

[18] English Translation – Was here

It Is Well With Mother

May 20, 1954 – January 31, 2018

"The hills come alive at the sound of music."[19]

January 1, 2018, Ivy Elizabeth Clarke watched one of her favorite classics "The Sound of Music." The hills around her house came alive as she sang,
"Do, a deer, a female deer,
Re, a drop of golden sun,
Mi, a name I call myself
Fa, a long, long, way to run…"
"Do, Re, Mi, Fa, Sol, La, Ti, Do, O! O!"

January 31, 2018, she was pronounced dead. The day after, however, My Heavenly Father reassured through His Word:

Ivy Elizabeth Clarke is not dead;
She is in Christ Jesus;
He is the Resurrection and the Life;
In Him she lives and moves and has His being.
So do not be discouraged!
Do not Fear!

---

[19]Wise, R. (Producer & Director), (1965). *The Sound of Music* [Musical Drama Film]. United States: 20th Century Fox.

Trust in the Lord
Live Your Purpose!

"Mom had many more years ahead of her!" I shouted

I agree,
My Heavenly Father responded.
But Ivy wanted to be with Me;
She gave forty-two years to education
And had a full life;
Do not be discouraged
She is now with Me in Paradise.

Ivy is still singing;
She has been made whole;
She is singing her favorite song
'It Is Well with My Soul.'[20]
Again
Do not be discouraged.
All is well!
It is well!
With Ivy's Soul.

She is not in pain!
She has not lost

---

[20]Spafford, H. (1873) It Is Well With My Soul [Composed by Philip Bliss]. In Gospel Songs No. 2 [Hymnal], Ira Sankey and Bliss: New York: Biglow & Main; Cincinnati: John Church & Co. (1875)

She has gained!
It is well!
It is well!
With her Soul!

If you could see her in Christ now
She is happy!
She is smiling as always!
She is singing
"It is Well with My Soul."

She now asks her family and friends, to
"Trust in the Lord with all thine heart
And lean not unto thine own understanding.
In all thy ways acknowledge Him,"
Only Him!
"And He shall direct thy paths."

"Be not wise in thy own eyes..."
Stop asking,
Why did this happen?
Trust in the Lord
And walk in your purpose.

Now rejoice and sing!
For all is well with Mother!
It is well with Ivy's Soul.

**Trust in the Lord with all your heart;
and lean not unto your own understanding.
In all your ways acknowledge him, and he shall direct
your paths.**

Proverbs 3:5-6

GLOSSARY

Asperger's syndrome - This is also called Asperger's disorder, is a type of pervasive developmental disorder (PDD). PDDs are a group of conditions that involve delays in the development of many basic skills, most notably the ability to socialize with others, to communicate, and to use imagination.
Asperger's syndrome. (2015) Retrieved October 29, 2015 from http://www.webmd.com/brain/autism/mental-health-aspergers-syndrome

Attention-deficit/hyperactivity disorder (ADHD) – This is a brain disorder marked by an ongoing pattern of inattention and/or hyperactivity-impulsivity that interferes with functioning or development. Inattention and hyperactivity are the key behaviors of ADHD. Attention-deficit/hyperactivity disorder (ADHD). Retrieved October 29, 2016 from https://www.nimh.nih.gov/health/topics/attention-deficit-hyperactivity-disorder-adhd/index.shtml

Down's Syndrome – A chromosomal condition that is associated with intellectual disability, a characteristic facial appearance, and weak muscle tone (hypotonia) in infancy. All affected individuals experience cognitive delays, but the intellectual disability is usually mild to moderate.
Down's syndrome. (2018) Retrieved August 21, 2018 from https://ghr.nlm.nih.gov/condition/down-syndrome#synonyms

Gazillionaire – noun (informal) A person who is enormously rich.
Gazillionaire. (n.d). Collins English Dictionary-Complete &Unabridged 10th Edition.
Retrieved October 24, 2015 from Dictionary.com website http://dictionary.reference.com/browse/gazillionaire

Grace - Short definition: favor, kindness. Definition: (a) as a gift or blessing brought to man by Jesus Christ, (b) favor, (c) gratitude, thanks, (d) a favor, Strong's Greek 5485 (charis) – grace. Retrieved October 24, 2015 from http://biblehub.com/greek/5485.htm

Gracious - 2603 chanan khaw-nan' a primitive root. To bend or stoop in kindness to an inferior; to favor, bestow; causatively to implore (i.e. move to favor by petition) beseech, (be, find, shew) favour (-able), be (deal, give, grant (gracious (-ly), intreat, (be) merciful, have (shew) mercy (on, upon), have pity upon, pray, make supplication.
Gracious. Strong's Hebrew Lexicon. Retrieved October 24, 2015 from
http://www.eliyah.com/cgi-bin/strongs.cgi?file=hebrewlexicon&isindex=Gracious

Refining
To purge or purify.
Refining. Strong's Exhaustive Concordance. Retrieved October 24, 2015 from
http://biblehub.com/hebrew/2212.htm

Salvation

3444 yshuw`ah yesh-oo'-aw ; something saved, i.e. (abstractly) deliverance; hence, aid, victory, prosperity:-- deliverance, health, help(-ing), salvation, save, saving (health), welfare.

Salvation (2015). Strong's Hebrew Lexicon .Retrieved on October 25, 2015 from http://www.eliyah.com/cgi-bin/strongs.cgi?file=hebrewlexicon&isindex=salvation

Tourette Syndrome (TS)

This is a neurological disorder characterized by repetitive, stereotyped, involuntary movements and vocalizations called tics.
Tourette Syndrome (2015). Retrieved October 29, 2015 from the National Institute of Neurological Disorders and Stroke.
http://www.ninds.nih.gov/index.htm

NOTES

Unless specified otherwise, all scriptures are taken from The Holy Bible, KING JAMES VERSION (KJV); public domain

"Submit the Letter..." (Page 9)

- Many are the plans in the mind of a man, but it is the purpose of the LORD that will stand. **Proverbs 19:21 (ESV)**

- Be anxious for nothing, but in everything by prayer and supplication, with thanksgiving, let your requests be made known to God and the peace of God, which surpasses all understanding, will guard your hearts and minds through Christ Jesus. **Philippians 4:6-7 (NKJV)**

- Be not wise in your own eyes: fear the LORD, and depart from evil. **Proverbs 3:7 (KJ 2000)**

- Be strong and courageous. Do not be afraid or terrified because of them, for the LORD your God goes with you; he will never leave you nor forsake you. **Deuteronomy 31: 6 (NIV)**

"Launch out into the Deep!" (Page 13)

- Now when [Jesus] had left speaking, he said unto Simon, Launch out into the deep, and let down your nets for a draught. **Luke 5:4**

- Read story in Luke 5:1-8

Your Purpose (Page 25)

- But Jesus beheld *them*, and said unto them, with men this is impossible; but with God all things are possible. **Matthew 19:26; Mark 9:23; Mark 10:27**

- As soon as Jesus heard the word that was spoken, he saith unto the ruler of the synagogue, Be not afraid, only believe. **Mark 5:36; Luke 8:50**

- I have glorified you on the earth: I have finished the work which you gave me to do. **John 17:4 (KJ 2000)**

- So when they had dined, Jesus saith to Simon Peter, "Simon, *son* of Jonas, lovest thou me more than these?"

  He saith unto him, "Yea, Lord; thou knowest that I love thee." He saith unto him, "Feed my lambs. He saith to him again the second time, "Simon, *son* of Jonas, lovest thou me?"
  He saith unto him, "Yea, Lord; thou knowest that I love thee." He saith unto him, "Feed my sheep." He saith unto him the third time, "Simon, *son* of Jonas, lovest thou me?"
  Peter was grieved because he said unto him the third time, Lovest thou me? And he said unto him, Lord, thou knowest all things; thou knowest that I love thee.
  Jesus saith unto him, "Feed my sheep."
  John 21: 15-17

Appreciate Your Calling (Page 29)
- Book of Jonah, chapters 1- 4
- A man's gift makes room for him, and brings him before great men. **Proverbs 18:16 (KJ 2000)**

Appreciate Your Gift (Page 31)
- The eye cannot say to the hand, "I don't need you!" And the head cannot say to the feet, "I don't need you!"
  1 Corinthians 12:21 (NIV)

- Do not be anxious about anything, but in every situation, by prayer and petition, with thanksgiving, present your requests to God. **Philippians 4:6 (NIV)**

Humility Essential to Walking in My Purpose
(Page 32)

- For this cause we also, since the day we heard it, do not cease to pray for you, and to desire that you might be filled with the knowledge of his will in all wisdom and spiritual understanding; **Colossians 1:9**

- Wherefore I also, after I heard of your faith in the Lord Jesus, and love unto all the saints, Cease not to give thanks for you, making mention of you in my prayers; That the God of our Lord Jesus Christ, the Father of glory, may give unto you the spirit of wisdom and revelation in the knowledge of him: **Ephesians 1:17**

- But he gives more grace. Wherefore he saith, God resists the proud, but giveth grace unto the humble. **James 4:6 (KJ 2000)**

- Humble yourselves therefore under the mighty hand of God, that he may exalt you in due time: **1 Peter 5:6**

- And he said unto me, My grace is sufficient for thee: for my strength is made perfect in weakness. Most gladly therefore will I rather glory in my infirmities, that the power of Christ may rest upon me. **2 Corinthians 12:9**

"Ask and It Shall Be Given" (Page 33)

- A man's gift makes room for him, and brings him before great men. **Proverbs 18:16 (KJ 2000)**

- Ask, and it shall be given you; seek, and ye shall find; knock, and it shall be opened unto you. **Matthew 7:7**

- And this is the confidence that we have in him, that, if we ask any thing according to his will, he heareth us: And if we know that he hears us, whatsoever we ask, we know that we have the petitions that we desired of him. **1 John 5:14-15**

- Trust in the LORD with all thine heart; and lean not unto thine own understanding; In all your ways acknowledge Him, and He shall direct your paths. **Proverbs 3: 5-6**

- Don't be afraid, because I'm with you; don't be anxious, because I am your God. I keep on strengthening you; I'm truly helping you. I'm surely upholding you with my victorious right hand. **Isaiah 41:10 (ISV)**

- But Jesus beheld *them*, and said unto them, with men this is impossible; but with God all things are possible. **Matthew 19:26; Mark 9:23; Mark 10:27**

- As soon as Jesus heard the word that was spoken, he said unto the ruler of the synagogue, Be not afraid, only believe. **Mark 5:36; Luke 8:50**

Exercise Your Faith (Page 34)

- Now the Lord had said unto Abram, Get thee out of thy country, and from thy kindred, and from thy father's house, unto a land that I will shew thee: And I will make of thee a great nation, and I will bless thee, and make thy name great; and thou shalt be a blessing: And I will bless them that bless thee, and curse him that curseth thee: and in thee shall all families of the earth be blessed. So Abram departed, as the Lord had spoken unto him; and Lot went with him: and Abram was seventy and five years old when he departed out of Haran. **Genesis 12: 1-4**

Trust His Strategy (Page 35)

- For my thoughts are not your thoughts, neither are your ways my ways, saith the LORD. **Isaiah 55: 8**

- **John 9:1- 41** – The story of Jesus healing a blind man.

"In God Put Your Trust" (Page 39)

- Abraham never wavered in believing God's promise. In fact, his faith grew stronger, and in this he brought glory to God. He was fully convinced that God is able to do whatever he promises. **Romans 4:20-21(NLT)**

- Romans 4: 13 – 21

Watch Me Work (Page 48)
- See "Think Wealthily - Stop Thinking Like a Pauper" in *Volume Two*.

- There is no fear in love; but perfect love casteth out fear: because fear hath torment. He that feareth is not made perfect in love. **1 John 4:18**

- Herein is love, not that we loved God, but that he loved us, and sent his Son to be the propitiation for our sins. **1 John 4:10**

Fear or Faith (Page 50)
- And we know that all things work together for good to them that love God, to them who are the called according to *his* purpose. **Romans 8:28**

- For we who have believed do enter into rest, as he said, As I have sworn in my wrath, they shall not enter into my rest: although the works were finished from the foundation of the world. **Hebrews 4:3 (KJ 2000)**

- The Lord is not slack concerning his promise, as some men count slackness; but is longsuffering to us-ward, not willing that any should perish, but that all should come to repentance. **Peter 3:9**

- But without faith *it is* impossible to please *him*: for he that cometh to God must believe that he is, and *that* he is a rewarder of them that diligently seek him. **Hebrews 11:6**

- And[Jesus] said unto them, Why are you fearful, O you of little faith? Then he arose, and rebuked the winds and the sea; and there was a great calm. **Matthew 8:26 (KJ 2000)**

- **S.T.A.R.R.S** - Acronym for Smart, Talented, Advisable, Respectful and Righteous Stewards.

Seasons (Page 52)

- There is a season for everything, and a time for every event under heaven: **Ecclesiastes 3:1 (ISV)**

See the Glossary for the meaning of *grace*.

This is Only Temporary (Page 54)

- My brethren, count it all joy when you fall into various trials; Knowing this, that the trying of your faith works patience. **James 1:2-3**

- *God* said to Abram, "Know for sure that your descendants will be strangers [living temporarily] in a land (Egypt) that is not theirs, where they will be enslaved and oppressed for four hundred years. **Genesis 15:13 (AMP)**

- But, beloved, be not ignorant of this one thing, that one day *is* with the Lord as a thousand years, and a thousand years as one day. **2 Peter 3:8**

- And I have led you forty years in the wilderness: your clothes have not worn out upon you, and your shoes have not worn out upon your foot. **Deuteronomy 29:5 (KJ 2000)**

- "At the end of every seven years you shall grant a release. And this is the manner of the release: every creditor shall release what he has lent to his neighbor. He shall not exact it of his neighbor, his brother, because the LORD's release has been proclaimed. **Deuteronomy 15:1-2 (ESV)**

- Now when the turn came for each young woman to go in to King Ahasuerus, after being twelve months under the regulations for the women, since this was the regular period of their beautifying, six months with oil of myrrh and six months with spices and ointments for women. [13] when the young woman went in to the king in this way, she was given whatever she desired to take with her from the harem to the king's palace. **Esther 2:12-13 (ESV)**

- For just as Jonah was three days and three nights in the belly of the great fish, so will the Son of Man be three days and three nights in the heart of the earth. **Matthew 12:40 (ESV)**
- And after fasting forty days and forty nights, he was hungry. **Matthew 4:2 (ESV)**
- "Thus says the LORD of hosts, 'The fast of the fourth, the fast of the fifth, the fast of the seventh and the fast of the tenth months will become joy, gladness, and cheerful feasts for the house of Judah; so love truth and peace.' **Zechariah 8:19**

Pruning (Page 56)

- I am the true vine, and my Father is the vine dresser. Every branch in me that bears not fruit he takes away: and every branch that bears fruit, he prunes it, that it may bring forth more fruit. **John 15: 1- 2 (KJ 2000)**

Refining (Page 57)

- "But who can endure the day of His coming? And who can stand when He appears?

  For He is like a refiner's fire and like launderers' soap. He will sit as a refiner and a purifier of silver; He will purify the sons of Levi, and purge them as gold and silver, that they may offer to the Lord an offering in righteousness. **Malachi 3:2-3 (NKJV)**

- And the very God of peace sanctify you wholly; and I pray God your whole spirit and soul and body be preserved blameless unto the coming of our Lord Jesus Christ. **1 Thessalonians 5:23**

- And be not conformed to this world: but be transformed by the renewing of your mind, that you may prove what is that good, and acceptable, and perfect, will of God. **Romans 12:2 (KJ 2000)**

- Be still, and know that I am God: I will be exalted among the heathen; I will be exalted in the earth. **Psalm 46:10**

- Who is this King of glory? The LORD of hosts, he is the King of glory. Selah. **Psalm 24:10**

See meaning of *refining* in Glossary.

Trusting in the Deep – Finale (Page 60)

- Now when he had left speaking, he said unto Simon, Launch out into the deep, and let down your nets for a draught. **Luke 5:4**

- For who has despised the day of small things? for they shall rejoice, and shall see the plumb-line in the hand of Zerubbabel; these seven are the eyes of the LORD, which run to and fro through the whole earth. **Zechariah 4:10**

- Let your conduct be without covetousness; and be content with such things as you have: for he has said, I will never leave you, nor forsake you. **Hebrews 13: 5**

Christmas is Here (Page 74)

- For God so loved the world, that he gave his only begotten Son, that whosoever believeth in him should not perish, but have everlasting life. **John 3:16**

- But he *was* wounded for our transgressions, *he was* bruised for our iniquities: the chastisement of our peace *was* upon him; and with his stripes we are healed. **Isaiah 53:5**

- But my God shall supply all your need according to his riches in glory by Christ Jesus. **Philippians 4:19**

- Then Jesus said unto them, verily, verily, I say unto you, Moses gave you not that bread from heaven; but my Father giveth you the true bread from heaven. For the bread of God is he which cometh down from heaven, and giveth life unto the world.
  Then said they unto him, Lord, evermore give us this bread.

And Jesus said unto them, I am the bread of life: he that cometh to me shall never hunger; and he that believeth on me shall never thirst. **John 6:32-35**

- For ye know the grace of our Lord Jesus Christ, that, though he was rich, yet for your sakes he became poor, that ye through his poverty might be rich. **2 Corinthians 8:9**

- Let them shout for joy, and be glad, that favour my righteous cause: yea, let them say continually, Let the LORD be magnified, which hath pleasure in the prosperity of his servant. **Psalm 35:27**

- Beloved, I wish above all things that you may prosper and be in health, even as your soul prospers. **3 John 1:2 (KJ 2000)**

- Charge them that are rich in this world, that they be not high-minded, nor trust in uncertain riches, but in the living God, who giveth us richly all things to enjoy. **1 Timothy 6:17**

- And the law is not of faith: but, the man that doeth them shall live in them. Christ hath redeemed us from the curse of the law, being made a curse for us: for it is written, Cursed is every one that hangeth on a tree: That the blessing of Abraham might come on the Gentiles through Jesus Christ; that we might receive the promise of the Spirit through faith. **Galatians 3:12-14**

- For he hath made him *to be* sin for us, who knew no sin; that we might be made the righteousness of God in him. **2 Corinthians 5:21**

- Bless the LORD, O my soul, and forget not all His benefits: Who forgives all your iniquities, who heals all your diseases, who redeems your life from destruction, who crowns you with lovingkindness and tender mercies, who satisfies your mouth with good *things, so that* your youth is renewed like the eagle's. **Psalm 103:2-5 (NKJV)**

- In whom we have redemption through his blood, the forgiveness of sins, according to the riches of his grace; **Ephesians 1:7**

- Therefore if any man be in Christ, he is a new creature: old things are passed away; behold, all things are become new. **2 Corinthians 5:17**

- To the praise of the glory of his grace, wherein he hath made us accepted in the beloved. **Ephesians 1:6**

- But God, who is rich in mercy, for his great love with which he loved us, Even when we were dead in sins, has made us alive together with Christ, (by grace you are saved;) And has raised us up together, and made us sit together in heavenly places in Christ Jesus: **Ephesians 2:6 (KJ 2000)**

- Nay, in all these things we are more than conquerors through him that loved us. **Romans 8:37**

- And ye are complete in him, which is the head of all principality and power: **Colossians 2:10**

- I can do all things through Christ which strengtheneth me. **Philippians 4:13**

- For who hath known the mind of the Lord, that he may instruct him? But we have the mind of Christ. **1 Corinthians 2:16**

- Christ hath redeemed us from the curse of the law, being made a curse for us: for it is written, Cursed *is* every one that hangeth on a tree: **Galatians 3:13**

- For sin shall not have dominion over you: for ye are not under the law, but under grace. **Romans 6:14**

- *There is* therefore now no condemnation to them which are in Christ Jesus, who walk not after the flesh, but after the Spirit. **Romans 8:1**

- Now it was not written for his sake alone, that it was imputed to him; But for us also, to whom it shall be imputed, if we believe on him that raised up Jesus our Lord from the dead; Who was delivered for our offences, and was raised again for our justification. **Romans 4:23-25; Romans 4:1-22**

- ...For if by one man's offence death reigned by one; much more they which receive abundance of grace and of the gift of righteousness shall reign in life by one, Jesus Christ.) Therefore as by the offence of one *judgment came* upon all men to condemnation; even so by the righteousness of one *the free gift came* upon all men unto justification of life. For as by one man's disobedience many were made sinners, so by the obedience of one shall many be made righteous Moreover the law entered, that the offence might abound. But where sin abounded, grace did much more abound: That as sin hath reigned unto death, even so might grace reign through righteousness unto eternal life by Jesus Christ our Lord. **Romans 5:17-21**

- As soon as Jesus heard the word that was spoken, he saith unto the ruler of the synagogue, be not afraid, only believe. **Mark 5:36**

Happy New Year – Write the Vision (Page 78)

- But he said to me, "My grace is sufficient for you, for my power is made perfect in weakness." Therefore I will boast all the more gladly about my weaknesses, so that Christ's power may rest on me. 2 Corinthians 12:9 (NIV) (The he is referring to The Lord)

Grateful to the Men (Page 82)

- Refer to www.thinkbabynames.com/meaning/1/Daniel

- For the LORD is our Judge, the LORD is our lawgiver, the LORD is our King. He will save us. **Isaiah 33:22**

- For the Father judges no man, but has committed all judgment unto the Son: That all men should honor the Son, even as they honor the Father. He that honors not the Son honors not the Father who has sent him. Verily, verily, I say unto you, He that hears my word, and believes on him that sent me, has everlasting life, and shall not come into condemnation; but is passed from death unto life. **John 5:22-24**

- Blessed is the man to whom the Lord will not impute sin. **Romans 4:8**

- There is therefore now no condemnation to them who are in Christ Jesus, who walk not after the flesh, but after the Spirit. **Romans 8:1 (KJ 2000)**

- "Therefore, if anyone *is* in Christ, *he is* a new creation; old things have passed away; behold, all things have become new. [18] Now all things *are* of God, who has reconciled us to Himself through Jesus Christ, and has given us the ministry of reconciliation, [19] that is, that God was in Christ reconciling the world to Himself, not imputing their trespasses to them, and has committed to us the word of reconciliation.[20] Now then, we are ambassadors for Christ, as though God were pleading through us: we implore *you* on Christ's behalf, be reconciled to God. [21] For He made Him who knew no sin *to be* sin for us, that we might become the righteousness of God in Him." **2 Corinthians 5:17-21 (NKJV)**

- Refer to behindthename.com/name/benjamin

- Hereafter shall the Son of man sit on the right hand of the power of God. **Luke 22:69**

- And Jesus said, I am: and you shall see the Son of man sitting on the right hand of power, and coming in the clouds of heaven. **Mark 14:62**

- For He made Him who knew no sin *to be* sin for us, that we might become the righteousness of God in Him." **2 Corinthians 5:21 (NKJV)**

- Behold, a virgin shall be with child, and shall bring forth a son, and they shall call his name Emmanuel, which being interpreted is, God with us. **Matthew 1:23**

- I can do all things through Christ who strengthens me. **Philippians 4:13 (KJ 2000)**

- And he said, The things which are impossible with men are possible with God. **Luke 18:27**

- But Jesus beheld them, and said unto them, with men this is impossible; but with God all things are possible. **Matthew 19:26 (KJ 2000)**

- See the poems "Be Like Joseph" in *Volume Two*
- Refer to http://nameberry.com/babyname/Joseph
- Refer to www.behindthename.com/name/Joseph

Grateful to The Ladies (Page 85)

- But the Holy Spirit produces this kind of fruit in our lives: love, joy, peace, patience, kindness, goodness, faithfulness, **Galatians 5:22 (NLT)**

- "And it happened after a while that the brook dried up, because there had been no rain in the land. Then the word of the LORD came to him, saying, "Arise, go to Zarephath, which *belongs* to Sidon, and dwell there. See, I have commanded a widow there to provide for you." So he arose and went to Zarephath. And when he came to the gate of the city, indeed a widow *was* there gathering sticks. And he called to her and said, "Please bring me a little water in a cup that I may drink." And as she was going to get *it,* he called to her and said,

"Please bring me a morsel of bread in your hand. "So she said, "As the LORD your God lives, I do not have bread, only a handful of flour in a bin, and a little oil in a jar; and see, I *am* gathering a couple of sticks that I may go in and prepare it for myself and my son, that we may eat it, and die." And Elijah said to her, "Do not fear; go *and* do as you have said, but make me a small cake from it first, and bring *it* to me; and afterward make *some* for yourself and your son. [14] For thus says the LORD God of Israel: 'The bin of flour shall not be used up, nor shall the jar of oil run dry, until the day the LORD sends rain on the earth.'" So she went away and did according to the word of Elijah; and she and he and her household ate for *many* days. [16] The bin of flour was not used up, nor did the jar of oil run dry, according to the word of the LORD which He spoke by Elijah." **1 Kings 17:7-16**

- You will keep him in perfect peace, whose mind is stayed on you: because he trusts in you. **Isaiah 26:3 KJ 2000**

Your Name and Purpose (Page 89)

- As for me, behold, my covenant is with thee, and thou shalt be a father of many nations. Neither shall thy name any more be called Abram, but thy name shall be Abraham; for a father of many nations have I made thee. **Genesis 17:4-5**

- And God said unto Abraham, As for Sarai thy wife, thou shalt not call her name Sarai, but Sarah *shall* her name *be*. **Genesis 17:15**

- And God said unto him, Thy name *is* Jacob: thy name shall not be called any more Jacob, but Israel shall be thy name: and he called his name Israel. **Genesis 35:10**

- Then Andrew brought Simon to meet Jesus. Looking intently at Simon, Jesus said, "Your name is Simon, son of John--but you will be called Cephas" (which means "Peter"). **John 1:42 NLT; Matthew 16:17-18**

- Acts 9

- Then Saul, (who also is called Paul,) filled with the Holy Spirit, set his eyes on him, **Acts 13:9**

Rare Diamond (Page 90)

- But my God shall supply all your need according to his riches in glory by Christ Jesus. **Philippians 4:19**

- The LORD *is* my rock, and my fortress, and my deliverer; my God, my strength, in whom I will trust; my buckler, and the horn of my salvation, *and* my high tower.
  Psalm 18: 2; Psalm 18:31; Psalm 28:1; Psalm 62:2

- Herein is our love made perfect, that we may have boldness in the day of judgment: because as he is, so are we in this world. **1 John 4:17**

I Am Loved (Page 93)

- And God said unto Moses, I AM THAT I AM: and he said, Thus shalt thou say unto the children of Israel, I AM hath sent me unto you. **Exodus 3: 14**

- So is the gift not like it was by one that sinned: for the judgment was by one to condemnation, but the free gift is of many offenses unto justification. For if by one man's offense death reigned by one; much more they who receive abundance of grace and of the gift of righteousness shall reign in life by one, Jesus Christ.) **Romans 5:16 -17**

Be Yourself and Walk in Purpose (Page 97)

- Trust in the LORD with all your heart; and lean not unto your own understanding. In all your ways acknowledge him, and he shall direct your paths. **Proverbs 3:5-6 (KJ 2000)**

- Every word of God is pure: he is a shield unto them that put their trust in him. **Proverbs 30:5**

- Let your conduct be without covetousness; and be content with such things as you have: for he has said, I will never leave you, nor forsake you. **Hebrews 13:5 (KJ 2000)**
- Be strong and of a good courage, fear not, nor be afraid of them: for the LORD your God, he it is that does go with you; he will not fail you, nor forsake you. **Deuteronomy 31:6 (KJ 2000); Psalm 94:22**

- And he said, Hearken you, all Judah, and you inhabitants of Jerusalem, and you king Jehoshaphat, Thus says the LORD unto you, Be not afraid nor dismayed by reason of this great multitude; for the battle is not yours, but God's. **2 Chronicles 20:15 (KJ 2000)**

- But the LORD is my defence; and my God *is* the rock of my refuge. **Psalm 94:22 (KJ 2000)**

Bi Tankful for Woo Yu Bi / Be Thankful for Who You Are (Page 98)

- I will praise you; for I am fearfully and wonderfully made: marvellous are your works; and that my soul knows right well. **Psalm 139:14**

- But by the grace of God I am what I am: and his grace which was bestowed on me was not in vain; but I laboured more abundantly than they all: yet not I, but the grace of God which was with me. **1 Corinthians 15:10**

Take Me Out of Your Box (Page 103)

- Whatever your hand finds to do, do it with all your might, for in the realm of the dead, where you are going, there is neither working nor planning nor knowledge nor wisdom. **Ecclesiastes 9:10 (NIV)**

- And whatsoever you do, do it heartily, as to the Lord, and not unto men; **Colossians 3:23 (KJ 2000)**

- For we who have believed do enter into rest, as he said, As I have sworn in my wrath, they shall not enter into my rest: although the works were finished from the foundation of the world. **Hebrews 4:3**

- And we know that all things work together for good to them that love God, to them who are the called according to *his* purpose. **Romans 8:28**

- The silver is mine and the gold is mine,' declares the LORD Almighty. **Haggai 2:8 (NIV)**

- For every beast of the forest is mine, and the cattle upon a thousand hills. **Psalm 50:10 (KJ 2000)**

- As soon as Jesus heard the word that was spoken, he saith unto the ruler of the synagogue, Be not afraid, only believe. **Mark 5:36; Luke 8:50**

- Herein is our love made perfect, that we may have boldness in the day of judgment: because as he is, so are we in this world. **1 John 4:17**

- Now when he had ceased speaking, he said unto Simon, Launch out into the deep, and let down your nets for a catch. **Luke 5:4 (KJ 2000)**

Dive Deeper in "...the Deep" – Finale (Page 111)

- But my God shall supply all your need according to his riches in glory by Christ Jesus. **Philippians 4:19**

- But God, who is rich in mercy, because of His great love with which He loved us, even when we were dead in trespasses, made us alive together with Christ (by grace you have been saved), and raised *us* up together, and made *us* sit together in the heavenly *places* in Christ Jesus, that in the ages to come He might show the exceeding riches of His grace in *His* kindness toward us in Christ Jesus. **Ephesians 2:4-7 (NKJV)**

- But he said to me, "My grace is sufficient for you, for my power is made perfect in weakness." Therefore I will boast all the more gladly about my weaknesses, so that Christ's power may rest on me. **2 Corinthians 12:9 (NIV)**

THE MOST GRACIOUS GAZILLIONAIRE SERIES

Volume Two
"My Grace is Sufficient for You"

A true story about "The Girl Who Lived Between the Hills and the Town" who uses poetry and dialogues combined with biblical verses to tell how her "Most Gracious Gazillionaire" freed her from "Religious Compulsive Behavior" (RCB) and taught her about her identity in The Lord Jesus Christ. He then used the poems "Be Like Joseph" and "Joseph and David: Purpose" to help with healing her emotionally from a divorce, and encouraged her to "Think Wealthily", "Speak Life" and take "Time to Meditate" on His gracious Word.

Volume Three
Experience the "Limitless Riches of His Grace"

"The Addict", "The Debaters", "Doubtful Minds", "Puzzled Mind", "The Fearful", "The Fearless", "The Thinker" and Gracious S.T.A.R.R.S eagerly waited to participate in a seminar with "The Teacher" who professed to know how to "Live the lifestyle of The Most Gracious Gazillionaire." After hours of poetic discussions on biblical issues, they were all stunned by the statements he made at the end.

ABOUT THE AUTHOR

Simone A. Clarke is a Jamaican who was raised in West Rural St. Andrew, Jamaica, between the hills of Above Rocks, Red Hills and Stony Hill. As she pursued her undergraduate studies in Hotel and Restaurant Management at the University of Technology, Jamaica, she began struggling with issues of fear. She began doubting whether she had chosen the right career path; however, she persevered. She graduated in 2002 while working as a pre-trained teacher of mathematics.

Ms. Clarke worked for seven years within her field of study. This included five years as a trainer in hotel and restaurant services. She did so along with volunteering to teach mathematics to youths at Church on the Rock, Kingston, Jamaica and completing post graduate studies in Adult Education at the Vocational Training Development Institute (VTDI), Jamaica.

In January 2012, Ms. Clarke left Jamaica to pursue graduate studies in Childhood Mathematics Education at City University of New York – Brooklyn College. During her first semester, one of her assignments was to write a mathematics storybook for children. Ms. Clarke wrote <u>Gigi's Encounter with Temperature</u>. By the time she graduated in 2014, her desire to research, write and educate both children and adults using the performing arts had soared.

Ms. Clarke found therapy in expressing her thoughts in poetry starting in November 2014. As she wrote, her desire to study the "Gospel of the Grace of God" (Acts 20:

24 KJV) deepened.

She succeeded in writing *The Most Gracious Gazillionaire* in three volumes:

Volume One – Be Yourself and Walk in Purpose
Volume Two – "My Grace is Sufficient for You"
Volume Three – Experience the "Limitless Riches of His Grace"

Ms. Clarke uses her poetry to assist with teaching "The Gospel of the Grace of God." Her pieces are also used to inspire others to "Launch out into the Deep," understand their identity in Christ Jesus and walk in their calling and purpose.

Connect with the author via social media:

- https://www.facebook.com/simonethespokenwordpoet.author
- http://www.instagram.com/simonespokenwordpoetry
- **Youtube:** Simone's Spoken Word Poetry or

  https://www.youtube.com/channel/UClaeQaTlbqwaHqGrBgBf7ww
- https://twitter.com/simoneswpoetry
- https://themostgraciousgazillionairepoetrybook.wordpress.com
- simoneaclarkethepoet@gmail.com

Many are the afflictions of the righteous: but the **LORD** delivers him out of them all.

Psalm 34:19 (KJ 2000)

Made in the USA
Columbia, SC
05 November 2022